Surf the Chaos with Style

Riding Life's Waves Without Losing Cool

Kottai Chezhiyan

ISBN 979-8-89699-799-3

GRATITUDE

Gratitude is the soul of this book, for no journey is ever walked alone. This work is a symphony of countless moments, inspirations, and lessons that have shaped and guided me. To everyone and everything that has touched my path, directly or indirectly, I extend my heartfelt thanks:

- Family, Extended Family, Friends, and Colleagues: For being the unwavering foundation of my life, offering love, strength, and values that anchor my journey.

- Teachers and Mentors: Thank you for sharing your wisdom, igniting curiosity, and relentlessly encouraging me to seek knowledge and growth.

- Books and Thinkers: For offering timeless wisdom, structured insights, and eternal teachings that challenge, inspire, and illuminate paths to greater awareness.

- Innovators and Artists: For daring to dream beyond the ordinary and crafting stories, music, and art that connect us to the essence of our shared humanity.

- Life and Nature: For being the ultimate teachers, revealing truths through joy, struggle, resilience, and harmony.

Above all, this gratitude extends to you, the reader. Your engagement breathes life into these words, transforming them from thoughts into shared meaning. This book stands as a tribute to the infinite influences that have guided this journey and a beacon for those seeking their own paths.

May the wisdom within these pages inspire and uplift you, just as it has for me.

CONTENTS

Introduction: Surf the Chaos with Style

Life doesn't come with a manual—it comes with waves. Some are playful ripples that tease your toes, while others are towering walls of chaos that crash over you, leaving you gasping for air. Chaos, in all its unpredictable glory, is life's only constant. But chaos isn't here to drown you—it's here to transform you.

The question isn't whether the waves will come—they will. The real question is: will you flail and sink, or will you rise like a surfer who knows the thrill of the ride? This book isn't about handing you a life jacket or magically calming the storm. Think of it as your surfboard and compass—a way to navigate the mess and emerge stronger, wiser, and unshaken.

Before we dive into the hows and whys of surfing chaos, let me tell you two stories from my own life—moments where chaos collided with transformation.

STORY 1: JUMP BEFORE YOU THINK

When I was eight, I watched my dad and cousins swim in a deep well. The water looked so inviting that I couldn't wait to join them. In true reckless fashion, I removed my clothes and leaped in, fully expecting to emerge victorious.

Instead, the water swallowed me whole. I panicked and nearly drowned. My dad, who happened to be underwater, pulled me out. I expected a slap—his usual fiery response to my antics. But this time, he took a different approach.

"You want to jump into the waters?" he asked, his voice scaring me. "Fine. But you're going to learn to swim first."

For the next 30 days, my dad threw me into every body of water he could find—wells, rivers, lakes, and even the sea. I hated every moment of it.

Every time I thought I was done, he'd make me do it again. But after that, I wasn't just a swimmer—I was fearless.

Now, I dive into wells for fun, pulling up stones from the bottom as my trophy. Looking back, my dad wasn't just my father during those weeks—he was my first *Vaathi* (which means "teacher" in Tamil). He didn't just teach me to swim; he taught me how to face fear and conquer it.

STORY 2: THE CHEMISTRY BIT PAPER

Fast forward to 10th grade. I'd just spent three months in the hospital with my dad, and when I returned to school, chemistry felt like an alien language. Salt analysis? Forget it. I decided to take a shortcut. Instead of studying, I crafted a micro-sized cheat sheet—a tiny piece of paper I was sure no one would catch.

But, of course, I got caught. My chemistry teacher, with sarcasm sharp enough to cut steel, praised my "creativity" in front of the class and then marched me to the school coordinator.

I was convinced I was doomed. But the correspondent didn't yell. She looked me in the eye and said, "You're brilliant in math. Why are you struggling in chemistry? I'll teach you."

For the next 20 days, she grilled me. Salt analysis became my life. She was relentless, drilling me until I could identify salts by sight and confirm them by smell. By the time I hit 12th grade, I didn't even need to study the subject—it was ingrained in me.

THE MEANING BEHIND KOLARU AND VAATHI

These two stories shaped the creation of *Kolaru* and *Vaathi*, fictional characters that represent two forces we all encounter in life. Their names are rooted in Tamil:

- Kolaru means chaos: the impulsive, disruptive force that creates confusion and resistance.

- Vaathi means teacher: the tough, unyielding guide who transforms chaos into clarity through discipline and hard truths.

THE COLLISION OF CHAOS AND ORDER

Imagine Kolaru and Vaathi in the same room. Kolaru's manipulative chaos meets Vaathi's no-escape discipline. Fireworks, right?

After one particularly disastrous stunt, Kolaru is sent to Vaathi. "This has to be a joke," he mutters, arms crossed, smirking as if he's already won.

Vaathi doesn't blink. "The only way out is through," he says, his voice calm but carrying the weight of thunder.

Kolaru thinks he's fighting Vaathi, but the truth is far more terrifying: He's fighting himself. His excuses, his fears, his deeply ingrained habits. Vaathi isn't just a teacher; they're a mirror, reflecting every uncomfortable truth Kolaru has been avoiding.

RIDING THE WAVES OF YOU

(MASTERING THE SURFBOARD OF SELF)

What if the key to thriving in chaos isn't about dodging life's challenges but learning to move with them—effortlessly, intentionally, and with your own unique style? "Imagine you're on a surfboard," Vaathi said, leaning forward with that familiar intensity. "You can't stop the waves, Kolaru, but you can learn to ride them. Or would you rather sit on the shore, watching everyone else figure it out?" Kolaru, never one to back down from a challenge, crossed his arms. "Fine, Vaathi. Teach me how to surf… metaphorically, of course."

Here's the truth: life doesn't slow down, and the waves of thoughts, decisions, and emotions keep coming. The good news? You already have what you need to handle them—your unique potential, values, and rhythm that make you, well, you.

The question isn't whether life will challenge you. It's whether you'll connect with the part of yourself that knows how to respond.

You might think you already know who you are—your quirks, habits, and goals. But if you've been feeling stuck, off balance, or caught in cycles that seem never-ending, it's time to ask deeper questions:

- Why do I hesitate just when I'm starting to move forward?
- Why does my passion sometimes feel like it's running the show instead of fueling it?
- Why does the idea of purpose feel so far away—like something just out of reach?

- Am I living a life that feels mine or one shaped by expectations I never chose?

This part of the book isn't here to rescue you. It's here to help you see yourself clearly—to understand your patterns, question your beliefs, and rediscover the tools you already carry within.

Life is an endless ocean of challenges and opportunities—waves that rise and fall, sometimes carrying you forward, other times threatening to pull you under. "So what's your plan?" Vaathi asked, arms crossed as they watched Kolaru wobble on an imaginary surfboard. "Plan?" Kolaru smirked. "I'll just let the waves decide where I go." Vaathi raised an eyebrow, tapping the stick in his hand. "The waves don't care about you, Kolaru. Master the board or prepare to drown. Your choice." The secret isn't controlling the ocean (good luck with that!) but mastering your surfboard: You.

We'll dive into practical questions that bring clarity:

- How do I cut through the mental noise and move with confidence?

- What can I do to balance my energy, curiosity, and goals so they work with me, not against me?

- How can I influence the world around me while staying true to myself?

Think of this as the moment you learn to tune into yourself. "Tuning in?" Kolaru scoffed, raising an eyebrow. "What am I, a radio?" Vaathi smirked. "No, but right now, you're all static. Let's fix that, shall we?" You'll confront truths you've avoided, challenge habits that keep you small, and step into the mindset of someone who moves with the flow—not force.

When you align with your rhythm, life shifts. Decisions become clearer. Obstacles transform into opportunities. And the voice inside you—the one that criticizes and doubts—starts to cheer you on.

The waves are calling. Ready to tune in? This is where the momentum begins.

Understand Yourself – Building the Foundation of Your Life

01

Life runs on an invisible system—a hidden blueprint made of your habits, beliefs, and experiences. This blueprint shapes every decision, reaction, and step forward. Most people never stop to examine it, staying stuck in patterns they didn't choose and scripts they never wrote.

Kolaru scratched his head, muttering, "Blueprint? It sounds like one of those diagrams engineers use. Why do I need that?" Vaathi's gaze didn't waver. "Because without it, you're living someone else's plan, Kolaru. Is that what you want?"

"Fine," Kolaru replied reluctantly. Vaathi continued, "This chapter is about uncovering that blueprint, questioning it, and reshaping it. When you understand how your mind works, you stop being a passenger in your life. You take the wheel."

STEP 1: DECODE THE PATTERNS RUNNING YOUR LIFE

Your thoughts and actions aren't random; they follow patterns. Some are helpful; others hold you back. Many of these patterns aren't even yours. They're hand-me-downs from family, culture, or society—like old clothes that don't quite fit.

Example: In The Matrix, Neo lived in an illusion shaped by a system he didn't question. Once he chose to see the truth, he gained power over his reality.

Exercise: Reflect on a decision where the timing was off. Identify thoughts or reactions that recur and ask:

- Where did this belief or pattern come from?
- Does it serve you, or is it time to let it go?

STEP 2: ALIGN YOUR VALUES WITH YOUR ACTIONS

Your values are your compass, guiding your decisions and keeping you grounded. When your actions clash with your values, life feels off-balance.

Example: Gandhi aligned every action with his values, inspiring millions. By contrast, Michael Scott from The Office often prioritized approval over authentic leadership, creating chaos.

Exercise:

1. Write down your top five values (e.g. growth, honesty, family, creativity).
2. Reflect on a recent decision: Did it align with those values?
3. If not, what needs to change—your decision-making, priorities, or goals?

STEP 3: CHALLENGE THE BELIEFS HOLDING YOU BACK

Limiting beliefs are invisible walls. They're not facts; they're stories you've internalized that keep you small.

Example: Katniss Everdeen from The Hunger Games doubted herself at first. By confronting her fears, she found strength she didn't know she had.

Exercise:

- Ask: Where did this belief come from? Is it really true?

- Rewrite it into something empowering: "I'm not capable" → "I'm learning and improving every day."

EMBRACE YOUR BLUEPRINT: THE LESSON OF YELLOWSTONE

In the early 20th century, Yellowstone National Park removed wolves, thinking it would eliminate a threat. Instead, the ecosystem crumbled. Without predators, elk populations exploded, vegetation vanished, and rivers eroded. When wolves were reintroduced decades later, the balance returned. Elks adapted, trees grew back, and rivers stabilized—not in spite of the wolves but because of them.

Lesson: The chaos we try to avoid—challenges, fears, and setbacks—often holds the key to growth. Like Yellowstone needed its wolves, you need your challenges.

Exercise: Instead of asking, "Why is this happening to me?" ask: "How is this happening for me?"

RECLAIMING YOUR BLUEPRINT

Understanding yourself isn't just about introspection; it's about reclaiming the driver's seat of your life. Your hidden blueprint shapes every step you take, but it's not set in stone. When you question your patterns, align your values, and challenge limiting beliefs, you're no longer just surviving—you're thriving. Remember, even the wolves in your life aren't enemies; they're teachers. Embrace them, rewrite your story, and move forward with clarity and confidence.

Kolaru leaned back, his arms crossed. "So, you're saying my habit of procrastinating on important decisions is like wearing someone else's old shirt?"

Vaathi nodded, unflinching. "Exactly. And that shirt doesn't fit, Kolaru. It's time to tailor your own."

"Fine," Kolaru muttered, scratching his head. "But next time, can we skip the wolves? They're giving me nightmares."

Vaathi smirked. "Only if you stop running from them and learn to lead your pack. Think about it, Kolaru."

FINDING FLOW – STAYING STEADY ON LIFE'S WAVES

02

Flow is the sweet spot between effort and ease—a state where passion propels you forward without tipping you over. It's about immersion, focus, and harmony with what you're doing. But here's the catch: passion, when unchecked, can burn too brightly, turning into obsession and leading to burnout.

This chapter is your guide to finding flow: distinguishing between passion and obsession, staying balanced, and building routines that turn passion into sustainable growth.

PASSION FUELS FLOW: HARNESS IT WISELY

Passion is powerful. It energizes, inspires, and drives growth. But without direction, it risks consuming you. Flow is passion with brakes—focused energy that propels you without burning you out.

"Flow? Sounds like one of those buzzwords motivational speakers throw around," Kolaru muttered.

"It's more than a buzzword," Vaathi replied. "Flow is where you stop being a spectator and start owning your life."

"Easy for you to say. You probably meditate on mountaintops," Kolaru smirked.

"Flow isn't about peace; it's about precision. Imagine balancing on a surfboard— not too tense, not too loose. That's flow," Vaathi clarified.

PASSION VS. OBSESSION: SPOT THE DIFFERENCE

Passion lifts you; obsession drags you down. Here's how to tell them apart:

Passion: Energizes, inspires, and brings balance.

Example: Serena Williams fueled her career with passion, balancing her competitive drive with joy for the game.

Obsession: Consumes you, isolates you, and makes failure catastrophic.

Example: Nina in Black Swan was consumed by perfection, sacrificing her well-being for an unattainable ideal.

Exercise: Reflect on a recent pursuit:

- Does it energize you or exhaust you?
- Is it enhancing your life or isolating you from it?

KEEP CURIOSITY ALIVE: THE OXYGEN FOR PASSION

Passion thrives on curiosity. Asking questions and exploring new perspectives keeps it fresh and exciting. Without curiosity, passion can stagnate or turn obsessive.

Exercise:

- What new skill, idea, or perspective could reignite your curiosity?
- Write down one thing you'll explore this week.

BUILD MOMENTUM WITH SMALL WINS

Flow doesn't happen overnight. It's built through small, consistent wins that create momentum.

Key Insight: Baby steps lead to big waves. Progress, not perfection, is the goal.

Example: In Rocky, every push-up and sparring session was a victory. The momentum came from consistently showing up.

Exercise: Identify a small, manageable action toward your goal. Repeat it daily.

BALANCE PASSION WITH SELF-CARE

Passion thrives when paired with rest and reflection. Self-care isn't optional; it's essential for sustainable success.

Example: Michael Jordan balanced his legendary intensity with downtime and personal relationships, keeping himself grounded.

Exercise: Create a "passion recovery" checklist:

- One activity that recharges you physically.
- One that nourishes you emotionally.
- One that inspires you creatively.

FLOW IS A ONE-WAVE-AT-A-TIME DEAL

Multitasking kills flow. Focus on one wave, one task, one moment at a time. Flow is about presence, not productivity hacks.

Pro Tip: Track distractions. Recognize what pulls you off course and create barriers to minimize them.

Exercise: Identify your top distraction and set a plan to reduce or eliminate it.

ALIGN PASSION WITH PURPOSE

Flow isn't just about how you work; it's also about why. Purpose gives direction to your passion, preventing burnout and keeping you grounded.

Example: In La La Land, Sebastian balanced his love for jazz with life's realities, finding fulfillment without losing himself.

Exercise: Write down your purpose in one sentence. How does it align with your current passions?

FLOW THROUGH IMPERFECTION

Flow isn't about smooth sailing—it's about adapting to chaos. Life throws rogue waves and unexpected challenges, but flow is finding grace within the mess.

Pro Tip: Breathe deeply when balance wobbles. It's your mental reset button.

Example: Surfers don't wait for perfect waves; they adapt to what the ocean offers.

CELEBRATE THE JOURNEY, NOT JUST THE DESTINATION

Perfection is a myth. Progress is what fuels sustainable growth.

Example: In Rocky, it wasn't about the title fight—it was about the training, grit, and the small victories along the way.

Exercise: Reflect on one recent achievement. What small wins led to it?

RIDE THE FLOW WITH PURPOSE AND JOY

Passion is your fire, but flow is how you tend it. Stay curious, stay balanced, and ride one wave at a time. The goal isn't just to move forward—it's to move forward with purpose and joy.

Kolaru leaned back, arms crossed. "So, flow is about one step at a time?" Vaathi nodded. "Exactly. Think less, do more. Flow isn't learned; it's practiced."

THE ART OF INFLUENCE – CREATING CONNECTION THAT LASTS

03

Master the subtle skills of trust, timing, and connection to build influence that inspires and resonates. Influence isn't about tricks or manipulation—it's about creating genuine connections. Real influence resonates by aligning trust, empathy, and timing to inspire action. This chapter unpacks the essential skills for influence that last.

TRUST: THE INVISIBLE FOUNDATION

Trust is the foundation of influence. It's earned through consistency and alignment between words and actions. Rebuilding broken trust requires humility and sustained effort.

Example: In Anbe Sivam, Nalla rebuilds trust with Bala by repeatedly proving his sincerity and commitment despite initial misunderstandings. His actions, not just his words, bridge the gap.

Pro Tip: Own up to your mistakes, apologize sincerely, and take clear steps to demonstrate change. Trust isn't restored overnight, but consistent effort speaks volumes.

"Trust is overrated," Kolaru declared, leaning back with a smirk. "If people don't trust me, that's their problem, not mine."

Vaathi raised an eyebrow. "Fascinating philosophy. Let me ask—when was the last time someone eagerly agreed to your idea?"

Kolaru hesitated. "Well… I mean, it's not like people are lining up to listen, but…"

"Exactly," Vaathi interrupted. "Trust isn't just a feel-good word. It's currency. Without it, you can talk all you want, but no one's buying."

"Fine," Kolaru muttered. "So, how do I fix it if it's already broken?"

"Step one: Admit you broke it. Step two: Show up differently. Every time you match your actions to your words, you deposit into the trust bank. And remember," Vaathi added, leaning forward, "One false move can wipe the account clean. No overdraft protection here, Kolaru."

EMPATHY: UNDERSTAND BEFORE YOU INFLUENCE

Empathy is stepping into someone else's world to understand their emotions and fears. Influence begins by meeting people where they are.

Example:

- In Sathuranga Vettai, the protagonist (unethically) exploits human greed by understanding what motivates people.

- In The Pursuit of Happyness, Chris Gardner's empathy for his son's needs drives his relentless efforts to improve their life, creating a bond of trust and love.

- Counterexample: When leaders overlook empathy, they risk alienating their audience. Tone-deaf corporate policies or product launches often fail because they miss what their customers truly value.

"Empathy? Sounds like emotional babysitting," Kolaru scoffed.

"It's not about babysitting," Vaathi countered. "It's about seeing the world through their eyes so you can speak their language."

STORIES: THE LANGUAGE OF INFLUENCE

Facts inform, but stories inspire. They bypass resistance, engage emotions, and make your message stick. A great story doesn't just explain—it resonates.

Example: In Soorarai Pottru, Maara's story of fighting systemic obstacles inspires not just his team but also his investors and customers. His struggles and perseverance are relatable, making his vision resonate deeply.

LISTENING: THE QUIET SUPERPOWER

Listening uncovers needs and builds trust. It's about understanding what's said and unsaid.

Example: In The King's Speech, Lionel Logue's ability to truly listen to King George VI allows him to uncover the root of his speech impediment and help him overcome it. It's this quiet attention that transforms their dynamic.

Pro Tip: Practice active listening. Paraphrase what someone says back to them. This builds clarity, shows you care, and makes people feel understood.

"Listening is easy. I just nod and wait for my turn to speak," Kolaru joked.

"Ah, the art of fake listening," Vaathi retorted. "Try actually hearing people out. You might learn something."

TIMING: STRIKING WHEN IT MATTERS MOST

The right message at the wrong time will fall flat. Timing is the bridge between intention and impact.

Example: In Visaranai, key moments of withholding or delivering information at the right time drastically change the story's direction and outcomes. Timing is critical, as the consequences of rushing or delaying become painfully evident.

"Think of timing like planting a seed," Vaathi explained. "Even the best seed won't grow if you plant it during a drought or flood. You need to wait for the right conditions."

CONFIDENCE WITH A TOUCH OF INTRIGUE

Confidence attracts attention, but intrigue keeps it. Striking the right balance between clarity and mystery engages curiosity and draws people in.

Example: In Iruvar, Anandan's charm and confidence captivate people, but it's his calculated intrigue and carefully revealed intentions that keep them engaged and supportive.

Pro Tip: Don't over-explain or push for validation. Let your ideas speak for themselves and leave room for curiosity.

BUILD A TRIBE: INFLUENCE THAT MULTIPLIES

True influence doesn't stop with individuals—it scales. When you inspire a group, you create a ripple effect that amplifies your impact. People want to feel like they're part of something bigger.

Example:

1. In Jai Bhim, Chandru's fight for justice doesn't just impact the people directly involved—it sparks awareness and creates a larger movement for change.

2. The team dynamic in Chak De! India shows how a shared sense of purpose and strong leadership can unify diverse individuals into a powerful collective.

CREATE WAVES OF CONNECTION

Influence isn't about pushing people; it's about pulling them into a shared vision. By combining trust, empathy, stories, and timing, you don't just create a momentary impact; you build connections that last.

"Influence? I can barely influence my cat," Kolaru quipped.

"Start small, Kolaru," Vaathi replied. "Even cats follow those who earn their respect."

By mastering these traits, you'll inspire not just action but a connection that lasts.

Self-Doubt Detox – Clearing the Fog from Your Spectacles

04

Standing at the edge of opportunity is thrilling, but self-doubt can cloud your vision. It whispers, "What if you fail? What if you're not good enough?" Here's the truth: self-doubt isn't a verdict; it's a fog—temporary, distorting, and entirely clearable. This chapter is your toolkit for cutting through the haze, challenging doubt, and replacing it with clarity, courage, and momentum.

SELF-DOUBT IS A DISTORTED MIRROR

Self-doubt often reflects a warped image of who you are, shaped by past failures, harsh words, or unmet expectations. You need to identify its origins and correct the distortion to move past it.

Example: In Good Will Hunting, Will's brilliance was hidden under layers of self-doubt, shaped by his upbringing and dismissive people around him. Confronting those beliefs unlocked his true potential.

Pro Tip: Self-doubt often carries someone else's baggage—don't let it define your worth.

"Self-doubt is like wearing sunglasses at night—completely unnecessary and obscuring the view," Vaathi quipped.

"I don't wear sunglasses at night," Kolaru shot back.

"Trust me, you do—metaphorically. Every excuse you make to avoid taking action is your version of shades in the dark," Vaathi replied.

Exercise: Write down three moments when self-doubt held you back. Ask:

- Are these beliefs true, or are they someone else's distortions?

REFRAME NEGATIVE SELF-TALK

The most dangerous critic lives in your head. Thoughts like "I'm not smart enough" or "I always fail" are just habits—and habits can be broken.

Example: Muhammad Ali declared, "I am the greatest," long before the world agreed. He wasn't ignoring reality; he was rewriting it.

Reframing in Action:

Negative: "I can't do this."→ **Positive:** "I've overcome challenges before. I can figure this out."

Negative: "I always fail."→ **Positive:** "Every setback teaches me something valuable."

- "You're good at reframing everything except responsibility," Vaathi teased.
- "I'm reframing this conversation as unnecessary," Kolaru retorted.

CELEBRATE SMALL WINS

Self-doubt thrives in the gap between where you are and where you want to be. Small wins bridge that gap, proving progress is happening—even if it's imperfect.

Example: In Rocky, it wasn't just the final fight that mattered—it was every punch, training session, and step up the stairs.

Pro Tip: Small wins are fuel for momentum. They remind you that forward is forward, no matter the speed.

Exercise: Write down one small achievement Vent daily, no matter how minor. When doubt creeps in, read your wins as proof of your growth.

TURN SETBACKS INTO COMEBACKS

Wipeouts happen—they're part of the ride. Every fall teaches you to paddle smarter, balance better, and come back stronger.

Example: Edison didn't see failure as defeat. He saw it as 10,000 lessons on what *doesn't* work.

Action Step: Ask yourself:

- What did I learn?
- How can I use it to level up?

This keeps the punch while making it cleaner and more direct. Let me know if you want any further tweaks!

HARNESS THE POWER OF VISUALIZATION

Visualization isn't wishful thinking—it's a mental rehearsal for success. By imagining your best outcomes, you prepare your mind to achieve them.

Example: Michael Phelps visualized every stroke, turn, and finish before stepping into the pool. By race day, his mind already knew how to win.

Exercise: Imagine your success in vivid detail:

- What are you doing?
- How does it feel?
- Who's there with you?

Use this image as a mental anchor whenever doubt creeps in.

SURROUND YOURSELF WITH GROWTH-ORIENTED PEOPLE

Your environment shapes your confidence. The right people challenge you, push you, and make self-doubt fade.

Example: In *The Blind Side*, Michael Oher thrived because he was surrounded by people who believed in him.

> *Kolaru sighed. "Man, I feel stuck. Like I'm running in circles."*
> *Vaathi smirked. "Maybe because you're jogging with people who never leave the track."*
> *"You saying I need to upgrade my circle?"*
> *"I'm saying growth is contagious. Get around people who are moving forward, and you won't stand still for long."*

Action Step: Identify three people who lift you up. This week, reach out—express gratitude, share a goal, or simply spend time together.

SEPARATE FEEDBACK FROM CRITICISM

Not all criticism is created equal. Constructive feedback helps you grow; destructive criticism holds you back. Learn to tell the difference.

Example: In Whiplash, Andrew Neiman filters the brutal feedback that pushes him to greatness while discarding what doesn't serve him.

Exercise: Ask yourself:

- What's useful here?
- What's just noise?

Write down one actionable step based on constructive feedback.

PRACTICE SELF-COMPASSION

You'll never silence self-doubt by beating yourself up. Self-compassion means treating yourself with the same kindness you'd offer a friend.

Example: In Inside Out, Riley learned that embracing her emotions—rather than resisting them—brought growth and clarity.

Exercise: Acknowledge the effort you gave and the strength you showed. Reread it whenever doubt resurfaces.

CLEAR THE FOG, SEE THE PATH

Self-doubt is like fog. It clouds your vision, but it's temporary. Clear it by uncovering its roots, reframing your thoughts, and leaning into small wins. The fog was never about your abilities—it was about your perspective.

"So, is this where you tell me to stop wearing metaphorical sunglasses?" Kolaru asked.

"Not just stop wearing them—stop putting them on others, too," Vaathi replied with a smirk.

"The fog is clearing. Your vision is sharp. The wave is here. Will you ride it?"

05

FINDING THE EYE OF THE STORM – MANAGING ENERGY, NOT TIME

Time is finite, but energy is renewable—if you know how to manage it. Chaos demands focus and strength, and even the simplest tasks feel overwhelming when your energy is drained. Einstein famously said, "Energy cannot be created or destroyed; it can only be changed from one form to another." This isn't just a principle of physics—it's a life lesson. By understanding and managing your personal energy, you can thrive even in the most chaotic storms.

YOUR ENERGY IS GOLD—STOP TRADING IT FOR LOOSE CHANGE

Energy is the currency of life. Spend it wisely, and it will take you far. Waste it on distractions or unnecessary battles, and you'll feel broke by midday.

Example: Nobel laureate Richard Feynman once said, "The energy you put into understanding something is the energy you get back." Focused energy creates a lasting impact.

Pro Tip: Treat your energy as sacred currency—invest it in pursuits that align with your goals.

"Sacred currency, huh?" Kolaru said with a smirk. "That's why I'm careful. I hoard mine like a miser."

"Miserly, yes. Wise, no," Vaathi replied. "Your energy isn't meant to sit idle. It's like water—stagnation only breeds decay. Invest it wisely, or it's wasted."

Exercise: Reflect on where your energy is going. Write down one unnecessary task or distraction you'll say "no" to this week.

PLUG ENERGY LEAKS BEFORE THEY DRAIN YOU

Energy leaks are the silent thieves of your productivity. Overworking, toxic relationships, and overthinking all poke holes in your energy bucket.

Example: Stephen Hawking said, "Work gives you meaning and purpose, and life is empty without it." But even meaningful work loses its spark when you're stretched too thin.

Pro Tip: Monitor where your energy flows. Are you investing it in meaningful pursuits or letting it seep into distractions?

"Energy leaks?" Kolaru raised an eyebrow. "Sounds like something out of a sci-fi movie."

"Reality is scarier than sci-fi," Vaathi countered. "Every time you overthink or argue unnecessarily, you're leaking energy. Patch it up, or you'll run on empty."

Exercise: Identify one energy leak in your life. Write down a specific step you'll take to patch it this week.

RIDE THE RIGHT WAVES: UNDERSTAND YOUR ENERGY RHYTHMS

Chronobiology, the study of biological rhythms, reveals that humans have natural energy cycles throughout the day. Recognizing your peaks and troughs can help you align tasks with your natural flow.

Example: Neuroscientist Daniel Levitin highlights that your brain's peak performance occurs in 90-minute cycles. Planning tasks around these rhythms can maximize productivity.

Pro Tip: Learn your body's energy patterns to ride the right waves of productivity.

"Riding waves? Are you teaching me surfing now?" Kolaru teased.

"Surfing energy waves," Vaathi replied with a grin. "Ride them right, and you'll thrive. Resist, and you'll wipe out."

Exercise: Track your energy levels for one week. Identify your most productive hours and align your most important tasks with those times.

SCHEDULE ENERGY, NOT TASKS

Instead of rigidly planning tasks, structure your day around your energy reserves. Focus on activities that immerse you fully rather than juggling distractions.

Example: Psychologist Mihaly Csikszentmihalyi, who coined the concept of "Flow", found that deep focus boosts productivity and creativity.

Pro Tip: Structure your day to maximize energy, not checklists. Flow happens when you're fully engaged.

"But what if my checklist feels sacred?" Kolaru asked.

"Then you're worshiping the wrong god," Vaathi said. "It's not about ticking boxes; it's about creating momentum. Prioritize energy and the list will follow."

Exercise: Identify one task where you can focus deeply without interruptions. Block time for it during your peak energy hours.

MASTER THE ART OF SAYING "NO"

Energy management isn't just about what you do—it's also about what you don't do. Saying "no" to unnecessary commitments protects your energy for pursuits that matter.

Example: Steve Jobs said, "Focusing is about saying no." Every "no" is a "yes" to your priorities.

Pro Tip: Saying "no" is self-care in disguise.

"I don't like saying no. It feels rude," Kolaru admitted.

"Think of it this way," Vaathi said. "Every unnecessary 'yes' is you saying 'no' to yourself. Who deserves the priority?"

Exercise: Write down one commitment you've been hesitant to decline. Practice saying "NO" to it this week and redirect that energy toward a meaningful goal.

RECHARGE RITUALS: THE POWER OF BREAKS

Even short breaks can restore energy and focus. Research by neuroscientist Andrew Huberman shows that activities like deep breathing or a quick walk reduce stress and restore balance.

Example: Einstein often took long walks to let his subconscious mind process ideas.

Pro Tip: Incorporate small recharge rituals into your day. They're more effective than powering through fatigue.

"Breaks are for the weak," Kolaru declared.

"Spoken like a true workaholic who's secretly burned out," Vaathi quipped. "Even machines need maintenance. Don't be a fool."

Exercise: Schedule a 10-minute break every two hours to stretch, breathe deeply, or take a short walk. Reflect on how it impacts your energy levels.

SLEEP: THE ULTIMATE ENERGY RESET

Matthew Walker, a leading sleep scientist, emphasizes that sleep isn't just rest—it's repair. Sleep strengthens memory, restores energy, and boosts cognitive function.

Pro Tip: Build a consistent bedtime routine to maximize the quality of your sleep.

"Sleep is for the lazy," Kolaru said, stifling a yawn.

"And ignorance is bliss," Vaathi snapped. "But neither will get you far. Sleep is where your body repairs its brilliance. Skip it, and you'll unravel."

Exercise: Evaluate your current sleep habits. Write down one small change you can make, such as setting a consistent bedtime or reducing screen time before sleep.

JOY AS AN ENERGY MULTIPLIER

Positive emotions expand your mindset and replenish energy. A moment of joy—a shared laugh, a beautiful sunset, or a kind word—can shift your energy instantly.

Example: Psychologist Barbara Fredrickson's "Broaden and Build" theory shows that joy builds resilience and replenishes energy.

Pro Tip: Seek small moments of joy every day. They're as essential as sleep or food.

"You're saying I should hunt for joy?" Kolaru asked.

"No," Vaathi replied. "Just stop ignoring it when it's staring you in the face."

Exercise: Write down one small moment of joy you experienced today. Reflect on how it made you feel and how it influenced your energy.

CHAOS MAY ROAR, BUT YOUR ENERGY LIGHTS THE WAY

Energy is your most precious resource. Protect it like a scientist guarding a breakthrough formula. Einstein said, "In the middle of difficulty lies opportunity." In chaos, managing your energy transforms challenges into possibilities. It's not about fighting every wave but conserving your strength for the ones that matter most.

HABITS THAT STICK – ANCHORS FOR YOUR PERSONAL SURFBOARD

06

Imagine standing steady on a surfboard in an unpredictable ocean. Waves rise, currents pull, and winds shift. What keeps you balanced? Your habits—small, consistent anchors that stabilize your life no matter what comes your way.

Good habits are like invisible compound interest: small investments that multiply into extraordinary results over time. But here's the catch: building habits that stick is tough. Motivation fizzles, distractions creep in, and routines crumble. The truth? Habits don't rely on motivation. They thrive on systems, intention, and discipline. This chapter will help you build those systems—making success not just possible but inevitable.

THE HABIT MYTH: WHY MOTIVATION FAILS

Motivation is overrated. It's like adrenaline: a sudden burst that fades just when you need it most.

Example: Every January, millions set ambitious resolutions. By February, most have abandoned them. Why? They relied on fleeting motivation instead of creating systems that make success automatic.

Insight: Willpower is like surfing without a leash—unreliable. On the other hand, systems keep you tethered, no matter the wave.

Pro Tip: Discipline isn't punishment; it's liberation. It frees you from chaos and impulsive decisions.

"Motivation's a scam. You can't trust it," Vaathi began.

"Well, I'm motivated to disagree," Kolaru shot back, grinning.

"Perfect example," Vaathi said. "That motivation will vanish by the time you form a proper argument. Habits outlive moods. Learn that or keep wiping out."

Exercise: Identify one habit you've struggled to maintain. Analyze your surroundings. Are they helping or sabotaging this habit? For example, if your phone is the first thing you grab in the morning, it's hijacking your focus. Make one supportive change today, like putting a book on your nightstand.

THE HABIT LOOP: HOW HABITS WORK

Habits are built through a neurological cycle known as the Habit Loop:

1. Cue: A trigger that prompts the habit.

2. Routine: The behavior itself.

3. Reward: The benefit that reinforces the habit.

Example: Brushing your teeth:

- Cue: Seeing your toothbrush.

- Routine: Brushing your teeth.

- Reward: Fresh breath.

Insight: Your brain craves rewards. Without them, habits fade.

Pro Tip: Anchor new habits to existing ones. For example, after brewing coffee, journal for five minutes. Reward yourself with the clarity it brings.

"A loop, huh? Sounds like a hamster wheel," Kolaru said.

"Only if you're running in circles," Vaathi replied. "When your loop moves forward, it's called progress."

Exercise: Write down one habit you already do daily. Link a new habit to it. For example, write down one thing you're grateful for after brushing your teeth.

START SMALL: THE 1% RULE

Big goals often lead to big failures. Why? They overwhelm. Instead, focus on small, consistent actions that snowball into massive results.

Example: James Clear's Atomic Habits highlights the "1% Rule"—improving just 1% daily compounds into 37x growth in a year.

Insight: Consistency beats intensity. Tiny actions done regularly outperform grand plans abandoned early.

"One percent? What's the point of such a tiny step?" Kolaru asked.

"Would you prefer to fall 100% flat instead?" Vaathi retorted. "Small steps get you there without tripping. The point isn't speed; it's staying on track."

Exercise: Break a large goal into one small action you can do today. Repeat it tomorrow, and let the momentum build.

THE FREEDOM OF DISCIPLINE: YOUR SHIELD AGAINST DISTRACTIONS

Discipline isn't restrictive; it's the ultimate freedom. It protects you from the endless noise of modern life: scrolling, binge-watching, or chasing others' priorities.

Example: Mahatma Gandhi said, "Freedom is not worth having if it does not include the freedom to make mistakes." Discipline isn't about perfection; it's about growing despite setbacks.

Pro Tip: Reclaim your time by setting boundaries. For example, "I'll check Instagram only after 6 p.m. for 20 minutes."

"Discipline is just a fancy word for rules," Kolaru muttered.

"Discipline is a toolkit," Vaathi corrected. "Use it well, and you'll build freedom. Ignore it, and you'll stay stuck."

Exercise: Write down one distraction you'll limit this week. Replace it with a habit that aligns with your goals.

OVERCOMING HABIT KILLERS: RESILIENCE, NOT PERFECTION

Even the best habits face setbacks. Focus on resilience, not perfection.

Common Habit Killers (and Solutions):

"I don't have time." → Attach habits to existing routines.

"I always fail." → Reframe mistakes as lessons: "I didn't fail—I learned what doesn't work."

"This is boring." → Add variety or rewards to keep habits engaging.

Pro Tip: Don't quit the habit; tweak the system.

"What if I fail at this habit thing?" Kolaru asked.

"Fail smarter," Vaathi replied. "Each stumble teaches you how to step better. The only true failure is quitting the habit altogether."

Exercise: Write down one habit you've abandoned before. Identify one tweak you'll make to its system and try again this week.

ANCHORING SUCCESS: THE POWER OF CONSISTENCY

Habits don't demand perfection—they require persistence. Small, repeated actions build momentum, snowballing into massive change.

Example: Surfers don't master waves in one day. They practice daily, honing rhythm and balance over time.

Insight: Consistency isn't about streaks; it's about showing up again and again, no matter how small the effort.

Pro Tip: Use habit tracking to visualize progress. Each tick on your tracker reinforces your identity as someone who sticks with it.

"But what if I miss a day?" Kolaru asked, fidgeting.

"Then don't miss two," Vaathi said firmly. "Consistency forgives a slip; it doesn't forgive surrender."

Exercise: Start a habit tracker for one small habit this week. Mark each day you complete it and notice the satisfaction of progress.

HABITS ARE PROMISES TO YOUR FUTURE SELF

Habits are more than routines. They're commitments to the person you want to become. Each small action, repeated with intention, builds stability for life's unpredictable waves.

"So habits are basically promises?" Kolaru asked, squinting.

"Not just promises," Vaathi said. "They're proof. Proof that you're not waiting for change—you're creating it."

As Sadhguru says, "Repetition is not about boredom—it's about mastery." The ocean will always be unpredictable, but with the right habits—your anchors—you can adapt, balance, and thrive no matter what comes your way.

WEATHERING LIFE'S STORMS

Life isn't all calm waters and golden horizons. Sometimes, it roars with storms—relentless, chaotic, and unyielding. The winds scream, the waves tower, and in the midst of it all, you ask yourself: **Can I hold on? Will I make it through?**

Here's the unshakable truth: **storms aren't sent to sink you—they're here to shape you.** They strip away illusions, test your resilience, and force you to master the waves that once seemed insurmountable.

Real surfers don't fear the storm. They meet it with steady eyes and determination, knowing that **chaos carries an invitation to ride higher, adapt faster, and emerge stronger.**

This part of your journey isn't about dodging the chaos; **it's about diving into it with purpose and resolve.** Together, we'll explore:

- How do you find balance when life feels uncontrollable?

- How can honesty and integrity guide you through the darkest tides?

- What does it take to turn wipeouts into comebacks and storms into strength?

The hardest lessons don't come from smooth waters—they're **forged in turbulence.** Storms will shake you, no doubt. But **they'll also show you who you truly are.**

What You'll Learn Here:

- **Face fears** that have held you back.
- **Turn setbacks** into tools for growth.
- **Embrace resilience** as both armor and fuel for your journey.

KOLARU & VAATHI ON FACING THE STORM

"You know, storms don't exactly scream opportunity to me," Kolaru muttered, kicking the sand with his toe. *"They scream 'run for cover.'"*

Vaathi smirked, tapping his surfboard. *"Only if you don't know how to ride. A storm doesn't wait for you to get comfortable, Kolaru. It demands you adapt. And in adapting, you grow."*

A REAL-LIFE EXAMPLE OF RESILIENCE

In 2011, Japan faced a devastating tsunami—a storm that leveled entire towns. Yet amid the destruction, **people came together, rebuilding stronger and more resilient communities.** They didn't just weather the storm—they used it to **innovate, adapt, and thrive.** Their story proves that even the darkest tides can carry the seeds of renewal.

With **faith as your anchor** and **adaptability as your compass,** you'll discover that **chaos isn't your enemy—it's your most powerful teacher.** Adversity isn't a signal to retreat; **it's an invitation to reinvent yourself.**

KOLARU & VAATHI ON REINVENTION

"Reinvent? Sounds exhausting," Kolaru said, rolling his eyes. *"What if I just stay as I am and avoid the whole storm thing altogether?"*

"Stay as you are, and you'll stay exactly where you are," Vaathi shot back. *"Storms don't wait for you, Kolaru. They move. And if you don't move with them, you'll get left behind or, worse, swept under."*

Consider This:

- What if you faced chaos head-on, without flinching or folding?
- How can you transform **every storm** into a stepping stone toward the life you want?

The answers won't come easily. **They'll be etched into your soul as you rise, fall, and rise again—each time stronger, braver, and more certain of yourself.**

KOLARU & VAATHI ON RISING AGAIN

"Alright, fine," Kolaru said, dragging his surfboard toward the water. "But if I wipe out, I'm blaming you."

"Blame me all you want," Vaathi said with a grin. "But when you rise again, remember: the storm taught you how."

YOUR MOVE

The storm is here, and the waves are rising. **Pick up your board, steady your stance, and paddle forward.**

Let's ride through the chaos—**together.**

07

CHAOS THEORY FOR SURFERS BALANCE IN THE SWIRLING TIDES—FIND YOUR CENTER AMID LIFE'S UNPREDICTABLE WAVES

Life often feels like riding a surfboard in a storm—waves crashing unpredictably, currents pulling you in every direction. Chaos can feel overwhelming, but what if it isn't your enemy? What if it's an untamed ocean that, with the right mindset, can teach you resilience, creativity, and purpose?

The right mindset begins with reframing chaos not as a force working against you but as the energy you can harness. This perspective fosters clarity, enabling you to see challenges as opportunities for growth rather than obstacles to fear. With focus and adaptability, the chaos transforms from a storm to a wave you can ride.

This chapter isn't about eliminating chaos (spoiler: you can't). It's about mastering it—finding balance amid the swirling tides and using chaos as a catalyst for growth and transformation.

CHAOS ISN'T A PIT—IT'S A LADDER

Chaos, like a ladder, presents challenges that also double as opportunities. Imagine a workplace scenario where a sudden project deadline disrupts your schedule. Instead of panicking, you assess the steps needed to meet the deadline, prioritize tasks, and enlist help where necessary. Each step up this "ladder" builds resilience and sharpens your problem-solving skills.

Similarly, a personal conflict might feel overwhelming, but by approaching it as a learning moment—communicating effectively and setting boundaries—you climb closer to personal growth.

To truly understand chaos, let's borrow the iconic words of Lord Petyr Baelish (aka Littlefinger) from Game of Thrones: "Chaos isn't a pit. Chaos is a ladder. Many who try to climb it fail and never get to try again. The fall breaks them. And some are given a chance to climb, but they refuse. They cling to the realm or the gods or love—illusions. Only the ladder is real. The climb is all there is."

Instead of fearing chaos, see it as the ladder Littlefinger describes. Assess the situation, take calculated risks, and climb steadily. Even if you stumble, the act of climbing teaches resilience. Chaos might shake the ground beneath you, but the ladder offers a way out—if you're brave enough to climb.

"A ladder, huh?" Kolaru mused. "What if the ladder topples?"

"Then you pick yourself up and climb again," Vaathi replied. "The fall isn't failure; it's part of the lesson."

THE OCEAN ISN'T OUT TO GET YOU

Chaos isn't a sign of failure; it's a sign of life. Those unpredictable waves—tasks, emotions, relationships—mean you're engaged, striving, and evolving. Instead of fighting the tide, learn to ride it.

Example: Think of Tony Stark in Iron Man. His chaotic lab wasn't an obstacle; it was the birthplace of his greatest innovations. Chaos, when embraced, becomes a playground for progress.

Pro Tip: Reframe chaos as raw energy waiting to be directed.

"So, chaos is just energy waiting for my brilliance?" Kolaru asked with a grin.

"If you're ready to harness it," Vaathi replied. "Otherwise, it's just energy waiting to drown you."

GOOD PROBLEMS VS. BAD PROBLEMS: CHOOSE WISELY

THE TRUTH ABOUT PROBLEMS

"Mark Manson taught me something most people don't want to hear," Vaathi began, leaning back slightly.

"Oh, this should be good," Kolaru interrupted, smirking. *"What profound wisdom did Mark bless you with this time?"*

"Life is essentially an endless series of problems," Vaathi said, ignoring the sarcasm. *"The goal isn't to avoid them—it's to pick the right ones. Happiness doesn't come from avoiding problems. It comes from solving meaningful ones."*

Mark Manson, in *The Subtle Art of Not Giving a Fk*, lays it out clearly: Good problems** challenge and grow you. They align with your goals and values. **Bad problems** drain you—distractions disguised as urgency.

GOOD PROBLEMS VS. BAD PROBLEMS

Good Problem: Training for a marathon—hard work, but meaningful. **Bad Problem:** Obsessing over office gossip—pointless and draining.

"So, if life is just problems on repeat, why bother solving anything at all?" Kolaru asked, his skepticism clear.

"Because solving meaningful problems is what makes life fulfilling," Vaathi replied calmly. *"Mark always said, 'The solution to one problem is merely the creation of another.' The key is to pick problems that are worth the effort."*

THE MOTIVATION TRAP: STOP WAITING TO FEEL READY

Manson also emphasized that **waiting for motivation is a mistake.** You don't wait until you feel like it—you act first, and the motivation follows.

✔ **"Don't just sit there. Do something. The answers will follow."**

✔ **"Action isn't just the effect of motivation; it's also the cause of it."**

✔ **"Something is worth doing, even if you don't feel like it."**

"Wait, so I'm supposed to just start even when I don't feel like it?" Kolaru asked, raising an eyebrow.

"Exactly," Vaathi said. *"If you wait for motivation, you'll never start. And some things,"* Vaathi paused for emphasis, *"are worth doing, whether you're paid, praised, or even in the mood for it or not."*

ACTION STEP: CHOOSE PROBLEMS THAT MATTER

Reflect on a decision where your timing was off and strategize for the future:

- **Does solving this align with my long-term goals?**
- **Is this worth my energy?**
- **If not, what can I focus on instead?**

KOLARU & VAATHI ON MAKING THE RIGHT CHOICES

"So, the takeaway is to pick the right problems and stop waiting for the perfect mood or moment?" Kolaru asked, leaning forward.

"Exactly," Vaathi replied. *"Life isn't going to hand you perfect conditions. The waves will come whether you're ready or not. It's your job to choose which ones are worth riding."*

SORT YOUR FIRES WITH THE EISENHOWER MATRIX

When chaos strikes, not all tasks are created equal. The Eisenhower Matrix, coined by President Dwight D. Eisenhower, helps you prioritize effectively:

	Urgent	Not Urgent
Important	Do it Now	Schedule it
Not Important	Delegate	Eliminate

Example:

- Urgent and Important: Tight deadlines.

- Not Urgent and Important: Daily workouts.

- Urgent and Not Important: Responding to group chats.

- Neither: Debating online about pineapple on pizza.

"Let me guess," Kolaru said, smirking. "Debating pizza toppings goes straight to 'eliminate.'"

"Unless your next job is as a food critic, yes," Vaathi replied dryly. "Otherwise, focus on what matters."

Pro Tip: Write tasks down, sort them into these quadrants, and focus on what matters.

"What if everything feels urgent and important?" Kolaru asked, exasperated.

"That's a sign you're overwhelmed," Vaathi replied. "Start by tackling what's truly urgent and important. Once you've cleared those, the rest will seem less critical."

BUILD SYSTEMS, NOT BAND-AIDS

Putting out fires feels productive, but it doesn't solve root causes. Systems prevent chaos from recurring.

Example: In Moneyball, Billy Beane used data-driven systems to transform his team. Instead of reacting to every problem, he built a system to predict and prevent issues, revolutionizing how baseball teams approach recruitment and performance.

"So, it's about setting up smarter ways of working?" Kolaru asked.

"Exactly," Vaathi said. "Otherwise, you're just stuck in a loop of fixing the same problems over and over again."

Exercise: Reflect on a decision where the timing was off and strategize a better timing for future decisions.

1. What's causing it?

2. What system can you build to prevent it?

"Sounds complicated," Kolaru muttered.

"It's not," Vaathi said. "Think of it like building a sturdy surfboard. You won't stop the waves, but you'll be better equipped to ride them."

MURPHY'S LAW: CHAOS HAS A SENSE OF HUMOR

"Anything that can go wrong will go wrong." Murphy's Law is life's way of reminding you to stay prepared.

Think of the classic scenarios:

- The projector died during your CFO presentation, even though you tested it five times.

- You wear a white shirt to an interview, only to be splashed with sewage water.

- Your laptop crashes with a blue screen of death just as you're about to send a critical email.

Murphy doesn't single you out—it's a universal phenomenon. The difference between surviving and thriving lies in foresight and preparation.

BUILD BUFFERS: FINISH TASKS EARLY

Buffer time is your secret weapon against chaos. Finish tasks early to absorb the inevitable surprises.

Example: Your train is delayed on the day of a critical meeting. With buffer time, you catch another train and still arrive on time.

HAVE BACKUPS: PREPARE FOR THE UNEXPECTED

Backups are your safety net.

- Save your presentation on a USB and cloud storage.

- Carry an extra shirt for surprise spills.

- Keep emergency funds for unplanned expenses.

Example: A student whose laptop crashes before an exam can recover if they've saved their notes in multiple locations.

"So, do I need to carry backups for everything?" Kolaru asked skeptically.

"Not everything," Vaathi replied. "Just the things Murphy loves to target."

STAY ADAPTABLE: FLEXIBILITY IS YOUR BEST DEFENSE

Even the best plans fail sometimes. Adaptability is your strongest shield.

Example: A presenter switches to a whiteboard when the projector fails, impressing the audience with their composure.

"Murphy strikes again," Kolaru sighed. "How do I win?"

"By preparing better every time he does," Vaathi said with a smirk. "Think of it as sparring with a tricky opponent."

SPEED READING: MASTER INFORMATION OVERLOAD

"Speed reading is a superpower," Vaathi began, tapping his desk for emphasis.

"Superpower? If I could have one, I'd pick flying," Kolaru quipped, leaning back with a smirk.

"Flying won't help you if you crash and burn because you couldn't get through the mission briefing," Vaathi replied sharply. "Speed reading isn't just about skimming pages; it's about processing critical information efficiently."

Speed reading is a versatile tool, helping you quickly assess the size and complexity of the "animal" you're trying to tackle. Whether you're a CEO, a student, or a general on the battlefield, it's about knowing where to focus your energy.

SPEED READING IN ACTION

1. CORPORATE SETTINGS

Executives often face lengthy reports, contracts, and market analyses. Speed reading helps extract key data points quickly, enabling informed decisions.

Example: A CEO preparing for a board meeting skims financial summaries to focus on areas needing attention, saving time for strategy.

"So, you're saying CEOs don't read every word of a 50-page report?" Kolaru asked.

"Of course not," Vaathi replied. "They focus on what matters—just like you should."

2. POLITICS

Politicians and diplomats navigate extensive briefs and position papers. Speed reading allows them to focus on policy impacts and critical clauses during high-stakes negotiations.

Example: During international trade talks, negotiators use speed reading to pinpoint contentious terms without losing track of the broader agreement.

"I'd probably just skim for the snacks section," Kolaru muttered.

"And that's why you'll never close an international deal," Vaathi shot back.

3. WARFARE

Military leaders process vast amounts of intelligence, tactical updates, and logistical data. Speed reading ensures they can quickly identify threats and prioritize strategies.

Example: A general reviewing battlefield reports uses speed reading to pinpoint crucial enemy movements while delegating other tasks.

"So generals are basically multitasking superheroes?" Kolaru asked.

"Superheroes who know how to read smartly," Vaathi corrected.

4. ACADEMIA AND RESEARCH

Researchers often sift through extensive journals and studies. Speed reading helps them locate relevant data to support their hypotheses.

Example: A scientist skimming multiple papers quickly identifies key findings and focuses deeper analysis on promising leads.

5. EVERYDAY LIFE

Whether tackling a mountain of emails or sorting through reviews before making a big purchase, speed reading helps prioritize what truly matters.

Example: Quickly scanning customer reviews to identify common patterns saves hours of indecision.

"You know," Kolaru said thoughtfully, "this might actually be useful for reading my boss's emails. Maybe I'll give it a shot."

"That's the spirit," Vaathi replied with a rare smile.

THE PROCESS OF SPEED READING

Skim First: Identify key sections such as headings, summaries, or visuals to get the gist.

Example: A student skims a chapter to locate formulas before diving into problem-solving.

Dive Deeper: Focus on actionable content relevant to your immediate goals.

Example: A manager highlights performance metrics in a report rather than reading every detail.

Review Trouble Areas: Spend time revisiting the most complex or challenging sections for a deeper understanding.

"This isn't about skipping depth," Vaathi emphasized. "It's about knowing where to dig deeper."

PRO TIPS FOR SPEED READING

1. Balance Efficiency with Depth

Speed reading is your strategy for assessing the "size of the animal" before deciding how to approach it. It's not about cutting corners; it's about prioritizing comprehension where it matters most.

2. APPLY IT EVERYWHERE

From textbooks to task lists, speed reading can transform how you process information.

"So, it's basically like knowing when to sprint and when to stroll," Kolaru summarized.

"Exactly," Vaathi said. "Because sometimes, understanding the terrain is more important than covering distance."

THE MARGINAL RETURN TRAP: WHY 80% IS ENOUGH

"Chasing perfection is like trying to carve a statue from a block of butter," Vaathi began, arms crossed. "Messy, exhausting, and likely to melt in the end."

"So, you're saying my obsession with flawless presentations is pointless?" Kolaru asked, raising an eyebrow.

"No, Kolaru," Vaathi replied with a smirk. "I'm saying you should aim for greatness, not perfection. There's a difference."

UNDERSTANDING THE TRAP

Chasing perfection often leads to diminishing returns—where every additional improvement demands exponentially more effort with minimal reward. It's the trap of doing too much for too little.

Reality Check: Perfection is expensive and exhausting. After reaching 80% mastery, every additional 5% demands disproportionate effort.

Example:

- 80% Mastery: High impact with reasonable effort.
- 100% Mastery: Exhaustion and unnoticed results—you're sweating over details no one cares about.

"So, stop ironing your socks," Vaathi added, "because no one's paying attention to them."

FOCUS ON WHAT MATTERS

Practical Tip: Stop at good enough and channel your energy into areas where you'll see meaningful results. Excellence is admirable, but efficiency is life-saving.

Life Application: Focus on tasks that truly move the needle. Whether it's work, relationships, or self-improvement, ask yourself:

"Is this extra effort worth the cost?"

"What could I achieve with the same energy elsewhere?"

"So, should I just give up when things get tough?" Kolaru asked, arms crossed.

"No," Vaathi said firmly. "I'm saying know where to stop. There's a fine line between striving for excellence and obsessing over irrelevance. Choose wisely."

FOCUS ON THE WAVE IN FRONT OF YOU

Chaos feels overwhelming when you try to tackle everything at once. Instead, focus on the wave in front of you—not the entire ocean.

Example: Surfers don't conquer the ocean in one sweep; they ride one wave at a time. Similarly, in life, narrowing your focus helps you manage chaos effectively.

Exercise: Reflect on a decision where the timing was off and strategize a better timing for future decisions.

- What was the wave you should have focused on?
- How will you prioritize next time?

"It's simple," Vaathi explained. "Focus on the wave you can ride now, not the one that might come later."

"That sounds suspiciously like avoiding multitasking," Kolaru muttered.

"Exactly. Multitasking is a myth, and chaos doesn't respect it either."

LAUGH AT THE ABSURDITY OF IT ALL

Sometimes, humor is the best way to deal with chaos. When the storm feels unbearable, finding its absurd side can help you regain perspective.

Example: In The Dark Knight, Joker's chaotic plans highlight an absurd truth: even the stormiest situations can have a comical twist.

"So, the next time my computer crashes during an important presentation, I should laugh?" Kolaru asked skeptically.

"Only after you've saved a backup," Vaathi quipped. "Murphy's Law is real, but it doesn't have to ruin your day."

THE 5-SECOND RULE: FROM THOUGHT TO ACTION

"The difference between action and inaction is often just five seconds," Vaathi began, tapping his stick on the ground.

"Wait, what? Five seconds? Is this a trick?" Kolaru asked, leaning forward suspiciously.

"Not a trick, Kolaru—a hack," Vaathi explained. "Five seconds is all it takes for your brain to sabotage a good idea or delay a critical move. But if you act before doubt creeps in, you override hesitation."

HOW IT WORKS

Coined by Mel Robbins, the 5-Second Rule is a simple but powerful tool to counteract overthinking and procrastination. Here's how it works:

1. The moment you feel the urge to act on something important—making a call, starting a task, or speaking up—count down from 5 to 1.

2. At "1," physically move. Stand up, open your laptop, or take that first small step.

"Counting down? Sounds silly," Kolaru muttered.

"It's not about the counting," Vaathi clarified. "It's about interrupting hesitation and replacing it with momentum. You're giving yourself no time to talk yourself out of it."

WHY IT WORKS

- Stops Overthinking: Your brain loves comfort and will rationalize staying in your safe zone. Counting disrupts this process.

- Builds Momentum: Action creates a ripple effect. Taking the first step makes the next easier.

- Increases Confidence: Acting decisively, even in small ways, strengthens trust in your ability to follow through.

EXAMPLE

Imagine sitting in a meeting, wanting to share an idea but doubting if it's good enough. The 5-Second Rule pushes you past hesitation:

- 5… 4… 3… 2… 1, you raise your hand and speak.
- Result? You contribute, build confidence, and overcome fear.

"So, it's like a countdown to bravery?" Kolaru asked.

"Exactly," Vaathi said with a smile. "And unlike your excuses, it works."

PRO TIP

Use the 5-Second Rule for small actions:

- Getting out of bed in the morning.
- Starting a workout.
- Tackling a task you've been avoiding.

"Five seconds to change my life?" Kolaru smirked.

"Five seconds to start," Vaathi corrected. "The rest is up to you."

Kolaru vs Vaathi:

Kolaru sat in the library, staring at his dismal 35% exam score, while Vaathi, ever composed, awaited the usual excuses. "The projector broke, my notes disappeared, and I didn't have enough time!" Kolaru lamented. Vaathi, unimpressed, dissected the situation. "Reading isn't studying, Kolaru. You didn't solve problems, review past papers, or test yourself. Flipping through pages is like surfing on land—it doesn't prepare you for the waves."

Vaathi explained the importance of SMART goals and focusing on high-yield topics instead of wasting energy on obscure ones. "80% of your questions come from 20% of the syllabus. You ignored the basics and weren't ready for setbacks," Vaathi said. Procrastination and cramming also came under fire. "The 5-Second Rule and timeboxing could've saved you," Vaathi added, emphasizing action over excuses.

In summary, Vaathi laid out a clear path: set specific goals, prioritize key topics, prepare for failures, and celebrate small wins. "Blame Murphy all you want," Vaathi concluded, "but stop giving him an open invitation."

Kolaru sighed, "Got it—next time, no excuses."

08 TRUTH BOMBS – STEERING STRAIGHT IN LIFE'S TEMPESTS

Truth is like Google Maps—it may frustrate you with reroutes, but it won't steer you off a cliff. Lies, on the other hand, are like those "shortcuts" your friend swears by, only to leave you stranded in traffic.

Sure, lying feels like an easy fix. Who doesn't want to avoid a tough conversation or skip owning up to a mistake? But lies come with a "Lie Tax"—a hidden cost that quietly drains trust, relationships, and peace of mind. Eventually, your web of lies collapses, and you're left trying to explain why your surfboard snapped mid-wave.

This chapter delves into how truth simplifies chaos, strengthens relationships, and prevents one from drowning in one's own fabrications.

TRUTH IS YOUR NORTH STAR

"Life's complicated enough, Kolaru. Why make it worse by pretending to be someone you're not?" Vaathi asked, tapping his stick on the ground.

"What if pretending gets you out of a tight spot?" Kolaru countered.

"Maybe for a minute," Vaathi replied with a sharp gaze, "but lies will pull you under faster than any wave. Truth, on the other hand, is your North Star—it doesn't waver, even when you do."

"Gandhi didn't just preach the truth (Satyagraha); he lived it—even when it was inconvenient. Spoiler: it worked out pretty well for him."

Pro Tip: The next time you're tempted to fudge the truth, ask yourself: "Am I steering by my compass or just winging it?" If it's the latter, don't be surprised when you crash.

The Cost of Lies: The "Lie Tax"

"Lies are expensive, Kolaru. They come with a subscription fee you didn't agree to."

Kolaru raised an eyebrow. "What does that even mean?"

"It means lies are like that streaming service you forgot to cancel—small at first, but over time, they drain your trust, relationships, and peace of mind," Vaathi explained.

Lies lead to:

- Lost Trust: Hard to earn, easy to lose.
- Broken Relationships: Lies chip away at the foundation until it collapses.
- Inner Turmoil: Your brain isn't built for keeping track of lies—it's built for survival. Lies make survival harder.

"Like Walter White in Breaking Bad," Vaathi continued. "He didn't lose everything because of cancer; he lost it because of lies."

Kolaru chuckled nervously. "So I shouldn't duct tape my surfboard?"

"Exactly," Vaathi replied with a smirk. "Lies are duct tape—they hold for a while, but eventually, you're just paddling in circles."

HONESTY SIMPLIFIES CHAOS; LIES AMPLIFY IT

"If chaos is a storm, lies are gasoline," Vaathi said. "They make everything worse."

"So, does honesty clear the storm?" Kolaru asked.

"Not clear it—defog it. At least you'll see where you're going," Vaathi clarified.

Example: Mark Zuckerberg in The Social Network could have saved himself years of lawsuits by being honest upfront. Instead, he surfed in the dark—and wiped out hard.

"Lies are like fog, Kolaru. You might think you're saving yourself some pain, but all you're doing is making the storm harder to navigate."

Jordan Peterson's Wisdom: "Tell the truth, or at least don't lie."

"Peterson nailed it," Vaathi began. "When you lie, you warp the structure of reality, and when it bites back, it's a dragon, not a mouse."

"So, lies don't just vanish?" Kolaru asked.

"Nope, they come back bigger and nastier," Vaathi replied.

Example: In Shrek, Fiona hid the truth about her curse, thinking it would protect her relationship. Spoiler: It made everything worse.

"Lying feels like a shortcut, but it's really just a detour to disaster," Vaathi said, leaning in. "Even when the truth is uncomfortable, it's always the safer path in the long run."

LIVING A LIE IS EXHAUSTING; TRUTH IS LIGHTER TO CARRY

"Lies are like juggling flaming sticks," Vaathi explained. "Truth is like juggling softballs—still work, but way safer."

Kolaru smirked. "Softballs don't sound so bad."

"They're not. That's why truth is easier in the long run," Vaathi said. "It's lighter to carry, even when it's uncomfortable."

Example: James Braddock in Cinderella Man was honest about his struggles, and this earned him respect—even in defeat.

"Lies require constant upkeep—what you said, to whom, and when. Truth? It just works."

TRUTH SETS YOU FREE, BUT IT MIGHT WIPE YOU OUT FIRST

"The truth might hurt, but lies cripple," Vaathi said, leaning forward.

"Great, so either way, I'm in pain?" Kolaru groaned.

"Yes, but one pain leads to freedom. The other traps you," Vaathi replied. "Choose wisely."

Example: In Dead Poets Society, Neil Perry faced the uncomfortable truth about his passion for acting. It wasn't easy, but it inspired others to embrace their authenticity.

"Here's the thing about truth," Vaathi said. "It feels like falling off your surfboard in front of everyone. But when you get back up, you're stronger and more aligned with reality."

TRUTH IS CHEAPER THAN THERAPY

Living authentically doesn't mean shouting your secrets from the rooftops. It means riding life's waves without pretending to be someone you're not. Lies may promise smoother seas, but they'll sink your ship eventually. Honesty stings in the short term but keeps you afloat in the long run.

09

RESILIENCE AFTER FAILURE – RIDING THE STORM

Life doesn't hand out perfect scores. It's a series of wins, losses, and everything in between. Resilience isn't about avoiding storms but learning to ride through them. Like a surfer knocked off balance by an unexpected wave, setbacks can leave you gasping for air. But storms don't last forever, and wipeouts aren't the end—they're invitations to rise, rebuild, and redefine yourself.

This chapter explores three phases of resilience: immediate recovery, long-term transformation, and bridging the gap between the two. Together, these steps will help you turn life's worst days into opportunities for growth and purpose.

SECTION 1: THE IMMEDIATE COMEBACK – BOUNCING BACK LIKE A PRO

1. EMPATHY FIRST: IT'S OKAY TO FEEL BROKEN

"Setbacks sting, Kolaru," Vaathi began. "Pretending they don't won't help. The first step to resilience is acknowledging what hurts."

"But if I just ignore it, won't it go away?" Kolaru asked, cautiously hopeful.

"No," Vaathi replied sharply. "It's like a bad wave—you either face it or get pulled under."

Example: Kapil Dev, criticized early in his cricket career, didn't suppress the pain. He channeled it into focus, leading India to a historic World Cup victory in 1983.

Pro Tip: Grieve, but don't linger. Processing your emotions is the first step to healing.

Exercise: Write about a recent setback. What hurt the most?

Reflect: Have I processed it fully, or am I carrying unfinished emotional baggage?

2. LIFE IS A GAME: EVERY POINT COUNTS

"Think of life like a tennis match," Vaathi continued. "You can lose points and still win the game."

"Roger Federer lost nearly half of the points he played but still won 82% of his matches," Vaathi added.

"Wait, he lost half?" Kolaru asked, incredulous.

"Exactly," Vaathi said. "His success wasn't about perfection but strategy and mindset."

Pro Tip: Adopt the "match mindset." Treat setbacks as part of the process, not the end of the game.

Exercise: Write about a "lost point" in your life. What did you learn, and how will it help you win in the future?

3. PRACTICAL TOOLS FOR IMMEDIATE RECOVERY

"Here's what you do after a wipeout," Vaathi instructed.

- Pause and Process: Take a moment to breathe, journal, or talk to someone you trust.
- Reframe the Narrative: See failure as feedback for growth.
  - **Example:** In The Karate Kid, Daniel uses challenges to build discipline under Mr. Miyagi.
- Celebrate Small Wins: Progress builds momentum.

SECTION 2: THE LONG-TERM TRANSFORMATION – TURNING PAIN INTO PURPOSE

4. THE PAIN PRINCIPLE: GROWTH IN DISCOMFORT

"Pain is your greatest teacher, Kolaru," Vaathi said. "It's a reminder that you're alive and building something new."

"Building what?" Kolaru asked, skeptical.

"Like a muscle," Vaathi replied. "Pain means you're growing stronger. Embrace it—but not the kind of pain that signals injury. That needs attention, not delight."

Example: Malala Yousafzai turned trauma into a global movement for girls' education.

Kamal Haasan once said: "Pain is a reminder that you're alive. It's the sign of building something meaningful. So, embrace it delightfully."

Pro Tip: Pain is inevitable; suffering is optional. Use challenges to teach, not break you.

Exercise: What is this pain teaching me? How can this discomfort help me grow?

5. THE YELLOWSTONE RESET: DISRUPTION DRIVES RENEWAL

"Remember Yellowstone's wolves?" Vaathi asked. "What seemed like chaos brought balance."

"So, setbacks are like wolves?" Kolaru quipped.

"Exactly. Sometimes destruction clears the way for growth," Vaathi explained.

Example: Steve Jobs, fired from Apple, founded Pixar and NeXT before reshaping the world with the iPhone.

Pro Tip: View setbacks as "ecosystem resets". They create space for reinvention.

6. LESSONS FROM LIFE'S STORMS

Lesson	Example	Pro Tip
Resilience is a muscle	Shah Rukh Khan overcame poverty to succeed.	Challenges strengthen you over time.
Adaptability is power	Chris Gardner survived homelessness.	Stay flexible—resourcefulness wins.
Gratitude fuels clarity	The All Blacks focus on humility.	Focus on what remains, not what's lost.
Find meaning in suffering	Viktor Frankl turned pain into philosophy.	Turn pain into a mission for growth.

SECTION 3: BRIDGING SHORT-TERM ACTION TO LONG-TERM STRENGTH

PRACTICAL FRAMEWORK FOR RESILIENCE

1. Process the Pain: Write a letter to yourself—honest, raw, and healing.

2. Build Support: Resilience grows through community. Reach out to mentors, friends, or family.

3. Track Progress: Use a "Victory Journal" to celebrate growth.

Pro Tip: Setbacks are plot twists—just hope your story isn't written by George R.R. Martin.

TURNING STORIES INTO STRENGTH

"Every storm leaves a story worth telling," Vaathi said.

Example: In Chak De! India, Kabir Khan turns public humiliation into a mission, inspiring a team of underdogs to World Cup glory.

Challenge: Write about your toughest experience. Highlight:

- What you overcame.

- What it taught you.

- How it can inspire others.

WAVES OF RESILIENCE

1. Resilience starts with feeling, healing, and rebuilding.

2. Pain signals growth and transformation.

3. Chaos often resets the ecosystem—use setbacks to reinvent.

4. Gratitude, adaptability, and community are your allies.

5. Every setback is a plot twist; how you respond writes the next chapter.

STORM RIDER'S INSIGHT

"Setbacks are opportunities in disguise," Vaathi concluded. "Pain isn't your enemy—it's your guide."

"When you embrace adversity, you discover strength, clarity, and purpose," Vaathi added. "The storm is fierce, but so are you."

10

FEEDBACK WAVES – ADJUSTING YOUR RIDE MIDSTREAM

Feedback—it's the love language of growth, though it doesn't always feel like love. Whether it's a manager critiquing your presentation, a teammate offering unsolicited advice, or a friend calling you out, feedback can sting. But here's the truth: feedback isn't about making you feel small—it's about helping you grow tall. Like a surfer fine-tuning his stance after every wipeout, the art of receiving and giving feedback turns rough waves into smooth rides.

WHY FEEDBACK MATTERS: THE GROWTH CATALYST

Feedback is the bridge between where you are and where you want to be. It reveals blind spots, sharpens your skills, and opens doors you didn't know existed.

Example: Michael Jordan didn't become the GOAT by basking in compliments. He actively sought feedback, dissected his mistakes, and used critiques as fuel for relentless improvement.

Pro Tip: Treat feedback as data, not drama. It's information to refine your approach—not a judgment of your worth.

Vaathi's Story: Fired at 18, Hired by Purpose

"When I was 18, I worked at a small pizza shop," Vaathi began, adjusting his stance for emphasis. "I thought it was a simple job—serve pizzas, smile, and go home. But I underestimated the discipline it required."

"Let me guess," Kolaru interrupted. "You ate all the pizzas?"

"No," Vaathi said, rolling his eyes. "But I did take unauthorized leave, showed up late, and acted like the rules didn't apply to me. My boss—a tough but fair guy—fired me within a month. His feedback was brutal: 'You're not fit for this job.' At first, it stung. I thought he was unfair. But when I reflected, I realized he was right. That moment redirected my focus. I wasn't built for that kind of work—but I had a knack for learning, strategy, and leadership. That firing planted the seed for who I am today."

"So, you're saying getting fired can be a good thing?" Kolaru asked, skeptical.

"It's not the firing itself; it's what you do with it. Sometimes rejection doesn't close a door; it redirects you to the right path," Vaathi replied.

THE STIGMA OF FIRING: WHY IT SHOULDN'T BE TABOO

Firing often carries shame, but it shouldn't. When done for the right reasons, it aligns potential with purpose. Misalignment harms both the individual and the organization.

Example:

- **Steve Jobs:** Fired from Apple, he built NeXT and Pixar before returning to revolutionize the tech world.

- **Dr. A.P.J. Abdul Kalam:** Career rejections redirected him toward groundbreaking contributions in space and defense.

- **Ratan Tata:** Early criticisms paved the way for Tata Motors' global success.

Pro Tip: Reframe firing as redirection. The end of one chapter often marks the beginning of a better one.

HOW TO TAKE FEEDBACK WITHOUT LOSING YOUR COOL

Receiving feedback well is an art. Here's how to master it:

- Pause Before Reacting: Silence isn't weakness; it's wisdom. Take a breath to process the message.

- Focus on the Message, Not the Messenger: Even poorly delivered feedback may contain valuable insight.

- Ask Questions for Clarity: Inquiry prevents misinterpretation.

Example: "Could you give me an example?"

Thank the Giver: Gratitude fosters trust and encourages future constructive feedback.

Exercise: Think about a time you received feedback that stung. Reflect on how you reacted and identify one way you could respond more constructively next time.

THE ART OF GIVING FEEDBACK: DELIVERING IT RIGHT

Feedback isn't about tearing down—it's about lifting up.

Four Golden Rules:

- **Be Specific:** Replace vague comments like "Do better" with actionable insights, such as "Your report could use data to support the conclusions."

- Use the Feedback Sandwich: Start with a positive, give the critique, and end with encouragement.

- Focus on Actions, Not Identity: Critique behaviors, not the person.

- **Empathize:** Help, don't hurt. Imagine yourself in their shoes.

FEEDBACK BEYOND THE WORKPLACE: A UNIVERSAL TOOL FOR GROWTH

Feedback isn't just for the office. It's a powerful tool in personal relationships, friendships, and family.

"Even kids have something to teach you if you're willing to listen," Vaathi said. "Their honesty might sting, but it can also be refreshingly insightful."

"Great," Kolaru muttered. "Next time my niece tells me I'm boring, I'll thank her."

TRANSFORMING FEEDBACK INTO ACTION

Feedback only works when you act on it. Follow this 4-step process:

- **Reflect:** Identify the core insight.
- Plan: Strategize how to address it.
- Act: Implement changes and monitor progress.
- Follow-up: Revisit the feedback giver and share your improvement.

Interactive Tip: Keep a 'Feedback Journal'. Track critiques, action plans, and results over time.

WHEN FEEDBACK HURTS: HANDLING CRITICISM GRACEFULLY

- Don't Take It Personally: Criticism is about actions, not your worth.
- Evaluate the Source: Not all feedback is valid. Assess the giver's credibility and intentions.
- Look for Patterns: Repeated criticisms often highlight areas for growth.

FEEDBACK WAVES: NAVIGATE WITH GRACE

Feedback, like the ocean's waves, may knock you off balance. But when you learn to ride its rhythm, it becomes a powerful force for growth. Whether at work or in personal life, feedback—when harnessed correctly—can guide you toward clarity, purpose, and mastery.

Take the feedback. Adjust your ride. And paddle stronger.

FAITH AND MEANING – FINDING ANCHORS IN TURBULENT WATERS

Faith isn't about **escaping the storm** but **finding your anchor** when the waves rise. It doesn't promise **calm seas** or a life without challenges. What it offers is **clarity, resilience, and the strength to keep paddling.**

Faith can take many forms—**religion, philosophy, or deeply personal convictions.** At its core, it's the quiet voice that whispers, **"This too shall pass."**

But faith isn't **passive.** It's not about whispering prayers into the void or sending wish lists to some divine hotline. **Faith is action.** It's the choice to **stand firm, live with integrity, and keep moving forward—no matter the storm.**

This chapter explores **how faith becomes both your lighthouse and anchor,** guiding you through chaos while unveiling your inner strength.

KOLARU VS. VAATHI: A LESSON IN ANCHORING

"Faith is for fools who can't handle reality," Kolaru declared one stormy evening.

"Faith," Vaathi countered, *"is what makes you stand when reality tries to knock you down."*

Kolaru smirked. *"If I trusted faith, I'd still be stuck waiting for someone to deliver my miracle pizza."*

"And yet," Vaathi quipped, *"the one time you put in effort instead of sarcasm, you actually got ahead."*

Faith's Sense of Humor: "I Asked for Strength…"

There's an old speech that pops up in reels and movies:

I asked for strength, and God gave me difficulties to make me strong.
I asked for wisdom, and God gave me problems to solve.
I asked for courage, and God gave me dangers to overcome.
I asked for love, and God gave me troubled people to help.
I asked for favors, and God gave me opportunities.
I received nothing I wanted but everything I needed.

Faith, it seems, has a **sense of humor.** Instead of **handing out prepackaged solutions**, it serves up **problems wrapped in messy, chaotic bows** and says, *"Here's your chance to grow."*

"Sounds like faith is outsourcing the work," Kolaru grumbled.

"It's not outsourcing," Vaathi explained. *"It's scaffolding—helping you build what's already within you."*

FAITH AS AN ANCHOR: TRUSTING THROUGH THE STORMS

Faith isn't certainty—it's trust. It's about stepping forward even when you can't see the full path and drawing meaning from the journey.

"Picture an anchor sinking deep into turbulent waters," Vaathi explained. "It holds your ship steady, no matter how wild the storm. That's faith—it grounds you."

Example: Viktor Frankl, in Man's Search for Meaning, found purpose even in a concentration camp. His faith in meaning didn't erase his suffering; it gave him the strength to endure.

STOP OUTSOURCING TO THE DIVINE

"Faith isn't just outsourcing miracles," Vaathi said, gesturing toward the horizon. "It's about embodying them yourself."

"Great. So, now faith is a DIY project?" Kolaru asked.

"In a way, yes," Vaathi replied. "*Aham Brahmasmi* teaches that the divine resides within you. Stop looking outside for what's already inside. Replace rituals of appeasement with intentional action."

Pro Tip:

- Instead of praying for strength, act with resilience.

- Instead of asking for peace, create it through forgiveness and understanding.

UNIVERSAL LESSONS FROM FAITH TRADITIONS

Across cultures and eras, faith traditions offer timeless truths:

Patience and Perseverance: Endure even when results seem distant.

Example: Nelson Mandela's faith in a free South Africa sustained him through 27 years of imprisonment.

Surrender and Trust: Letting go often brings clarity.

Example: The Bhagavad Gita teaches focusing on effort, not outcomes.

Mindfulness and Presence: Live fully in the moment.

Example: Zen Buddhism's wisdom: "Let go or be dragged."

Forgiveness and Compassion: Forgiveness liberates you from resentment.

Example: Christianity emphasizes forgiveness as a path to inner peace.

FAITH AND DOUBT: NECESSARY COMPANIONS

"Faith without doubt is blind," Vaathi remarked. "And doubt without faith is lost."

"Let me guess," Kolaru said, "you're about to say they're best friends?"

"Not quite," Vaathi smiled. "But they're necessary companions. Doubt sharpens faith, forcing you to discard assumptions and build something stronger."

FAITH IN ACTION: TOOLS FOR RESILIENCE

Faith becomes real when it translates into action. Here are simple steps to ground yourself:

1. Anchor in the Moment: Sip tea, journal, or walk mindfully for five minutes.
2. Draw Strength from Stories: Reflect on personal or historical examples of resilience.
3. Build a Support System: Engage with people or communities that uplift you.

RELIGION AS CONTEXT, NOT ABSOLUTE TRUTH

Religious texts are like historical "Wikipedia" filled with wisdom but shaped by their era. While much of their insight remains timeless, specifics often don't.

"Burning or dismissing texts doesn't erase history," Vaathi warned. "It destroys bridges to wisdom."

Pro Tip: Treat texts as guides, not gospel. Extract their wisdom and discard outdated practices.

THE CALM WITHIN THE CHAOS

Faith doesn't remove life's storms; it changes how you face them. It shifts your perspective from despair to determination, reminding you that calm, clarity, and courage are already within you—waiting to be discovered.

"Storms will pass," Vaathi said. "But the strength you build will stay."

REFLECTION CHALLENGE

- What storm are you currently weathering?
- How can your faith—whether in yourself, humanity, or a higher power—anchor you through it?

WAVES OF FAITH

1. Faith grounds you during chaos, reminding you that storms pass.
2. Doubt complements faith, sharpening its strength.
3. Meaning turns suffering into purpose.
4. Gratitude and presence transform your perspective.
5. Faith, in action, is the ultimate resilience tool.

FAITH STEADIES, CHAOS TESTS, YOU CONQUER

"Faith isn't about waiting for calmer seas," Vaathi concluded. "It's about finding the strength to paddle forward, even when the waves rise."

"Looks like faith might be worth a shot," Kolaru admitted.

"Faith isn't a shot, Kolaru," Vaathi replied. "It's your anchor."

Kolaru leaned back, smirking. "Alright, Vaathi, what if I don't believe in God? Where's this so-called anchor supposed to come from then?"

Vaathi didn't flinch. "Faith isn't limited to God, Kolaru," he said, leaning forward. "It's about trust—whether it is in a higher power, humanity, science, or even yourself. Faith is the act of grounding yourself in something bigger than your current struggle."

Kolaru raised an eyebrow. "So, I can have faith in… me?"

"Absolutely," Vaathi replied. "Belief in yourself is one of the strongest anchors. Faith doesn't need a deity; it needs conviction. Viktor Frankl survived a concentration camp by finding meaning in his suffering, not by relying on divine intervention. His anchor was his purpose, not a God."

"But what if everything around me just feels… meaningless?" Kolaru asked, his voice quieter this time.

Vaathi's expression softened. "Then start small. Find meaning in the little things—a good book, a challenge to overcome, a person to support. This means it grows like roots, Kolaru, and it doesn't matter where you plant it. Whether your faith is in a divine force, logic, or the simple hope that tomorrow will be better, what matters is that it steadies you."

"So, faith is just… choosing not to give up?" Kolaru ventured.

"Not quite," Vaathi said, smiling. "Faith is choosing to move forward, even when you're unsure of the outcome. It's trusting that the storm will pass and that you'll come out stronger on the other side—whether or not you believe in God."

Kolaru furrowed his brow, still skeptical. "Alright, fine. Maybe there's something to this faith thing, even if it doesn't involve some bearded guy in the clouds. But let's be real—what difference does it actually make? I'm still here, stuck in my chaos."

Vaathi chuckled, his tone sharper now. "And why do you think you're stuck, Kolaru? It's because you didn't have faith in yourself earlier. You've been beaten down by life, not because of the storms, but because you refused to trust your own ability to navigate them."

Kolaru blinked, taken aback. "Wait, are you saying this is all my fault?"

Vaathi's gaze was piercing. "Not your fault—your choice. You chose doubt over trust, hesitation over action, and excuses over resilience. If you'd had faith in yourself from the start, you'd have paddled through the storm instead of letting it toss you around like driftwood."

"But I didn't know how!" Kolaru protested, his voice rising defensively.

"And whose job was it to figure it out?" Vaathi shot back, his voice unwavering. "Faith isn't about having all the answers—it's about trusting that you'll find them. You spent more time questioning the storm than learning how to ride its waves. That's why you're getting beaten, Kolaru—not by me, but by your own unwillingness to believe in yourself."

For once, Kolaru had no witty retort. He slumped back in his seat, eyes downcast. "So, what do I do now?"

Vaathi's tone softened, but the steel in his words remained. "You start now. You find one thing to anchor yourself to—a goal, a principle, a small win. And you commit to it with faith, not doubt. The storms will keep coming, Kolaru, but with faith in yourself, you won't just survive them; you'll ride them."

Kolaru sat silently for a moment, then muttered, "So, I've been paddling in circles, huh?"

"Exactly," Vaathi said with a rare smirk. "And you're getting beaten by me because you didn't believe in yourself earlier. But the beating isn't the end— it's the beginning. Now, pick up that board and start paddling forward."

Navigating Gen Z's Unique and Timeless Challenges

12

You, dear reader, are living through an era of unparalleled paradoxes. You're hyperconnected yet lonely, surrounded by infinite possibilities yet burdened by the pressure to seize them all. While individuality is celebrated in every headline, the world subtly nudges you toward conformity. Navigating these waves is no small feat, but here's the secret: the storms you face today—identity, success, connection, and meaning—are as old as time, just wearing trendier clothes.

This chapter dissects Gen Z's unique struggles while anchoring them in timeless wisdom, offering a path forward to surf these waves with resilience, purpose, and clarity.

THE SOCIAL MEDIA CARNIVAL: MIRRORS, MASKS, AND METRICS

Social media is the modern town square—equal parts connection and competition. It's not only a tool of inspiration but also a factory of comparison. Highlight reels masquerade as reality, amplifying anxiety and a sense of inadequacy.

"Your worth isn't defined by likes, followers, or comments," Vaathi said firmly. "Social media is a tool, not your mirror. If you're letting it reflect who you are, you're surfing with a cracked board."

"Fine, but what do I do then?" Kolaru sighed.

"Curate your feed. Unfollow anything that drains you. Fill it with people, ideas, and stories that inspire growth. Social media can either be a spotlight or a shadow—it's up to you to decide which it will be."

Action Step:

- Audit your social media feed.

- Unfollow accounts that trigger anxiety or unhealthy comparisons.

- Follow pages that inspire creativity, joy, and growth.

FREEDOM ISN'T FREE: BALANCING ASPIRATIONS AND RESPONSIBILITIES

Gen Z's freedom comes with a silent burden: decision fatigue. Careers are no longer ladders—they're jungle gyms offering multi-directional paths that excite and overwhelm in equal measure.

"Freedom doesn't mean saying yes to everything," Vaathi explained. "Every yes is a no to something else. True liberation lies in knowing what to say no to."

"So, do we just make choices and hope for the best?" Kolaru quipped.

"No," Vaathi said. "You set boundaries and align your choices with your values. That's how you create freedom within structure."

Action Step:

- Write down three core priorities (e.g. health, family, creativity).

- Compare them to your daily schedule. Are you investing time in what matters?

MENTAL HEALTH IN THE SPOTLIGHT: FROM STIGMA TO STRENGTH

Gen Z has led the charge in destigmatizing mental health. Therapy is no longer taboo—it's a strength. But awareness is just the starting point; consistency is the real journey.

"Your mind is like a garden," Vaathi said. "You have to water what grows and pull out what doesn't. Daily practices like journaling or mindfulness are the tools that keep your garden thriving."

"What if I don't have time?" Kolaru mumbled.

Vaathi shot him a look. "You make time, Kolaru. Ten minutes a day is all it takes to turn chaos into calm."

Action Step:

- Dedicate 10 minutes daily to a self-care practice: gratitude journaling, deep breathing, or screen-free time.

THE EARTH'S CRY: FROM ANXIETY TO ACTION

Climate change isn't an abstract problem for Gen Z—it's their reality. But the enormity of the issue often feels paralyzing.

"Big change starts small," Vaathi reminded. "Greta Thunberg didn't wake up one day and fix the world. She started with a sign and a protest. Small actions, multiplied, create massive change."

"What's one thing I can do?" Kolaru asked.

"Start where you are. Plant a tree, cut down your waste, or educate yourself. Progress beats paralysis every time."

REDEFINING SUCCESS: BEYOND METRICS AND MILESTONES

The obsession with metrics—likes, salaries, grades—can trap you in a cycle of external validation.

"Success isn't about numbers," Vaathi said. "It's about alignment. Are you living in line with your values? That's a success."

"So, you're saying rest is okay?" Kolaru asked cautiously.

"Rest isn't just okay—it's essential. Sometimes, stepping back is the only way to move forward."

Action Step:

- Schedule rest as you would any other priority. Treat it as non-negotiable.

THE POWER OF CONNECTION: DEPTH OVER BREADTH

Hyperconnectivity has made loneliness paradoxical. Hundreds of contacts but few meaningful conversations.

"Connection isn't about how many people you know," Vaathi said. "It's about the depth of your roots. Invest in conversations that matter."

Action Step:

- Reach out to one friend today for a meaningful conversation.

THE WISDOM OF FAILURE: TURNING STUMBLES INTO STRENGTH

Failure feels magnified in a hyperconnected world, where every stumble feels meme-worthy.

"Failure isn't the end," Vaathi said, his voice firm. "It's feedback. If you're afraid to fail, you'll never try. And if you never try, you'll never know what you're capable of."

"But what if everyone's watching?" Kolaru muttered.

"Let them watch," Vaathi replied with a grin. "Your worst day could be the foundation of your greatest triumph. The audience doesn't matter—your growth does."

Action Challenge:

- Write about a recent failure. Identify one lesson and one way it redirected your path.

OWNING YOUR JOURNEY: SURFING YOUR UNIQUE WAVES

The challenges you face are real, but they're not insurmountable. They're the same storms humanity has always braved; however, they are now wrapped in modern dilemmas.

"What defines you isn't the obstacles," Vaathi said. "It's how you navigate them. Choose courage over comparison, depth over distractions, and meaning over metrics."

Closing Visual: Picture your life as a surfboard on vast, unpredictable waves. The tides may pull you in every direction, but you'll find your rhythm with balance, purpose, and trust.

NAVIGATING GEN Z'S CHALLENGES

1. Social media is a tool, not a mirror—curate it wisely.

2. Freedom lies in boundaries, not endless choices.

3. Mental health requires daily care; it's a strength, not a stigma.

4. Small actions multiplied create massive change.

5. Success isn't a ladder; it's a winding path.

6. Failure isn't defeat—it's feedback.

GEN Z DOESN'T JUST SURF WAVES—THEY SHAPE OCEANS

Your generation is rewriting the rules, reshaping culture, and challenging norms. Ride the waves with intention, clarity, and courage. The ocean is vast, and the tides are unpredictable, but you are limitless.

CONNECTING IN THE FLOW – CATCHING THE RIGHT WAVES TOGETHER

(PEOPLE: CAN'T LIVE WITH THEM, CAN'T LIVE WITHOUT THEM)

Connection is the invisible thread that stitches meaning into life. Yet, in an era of **hyperconnectivity**, it's the very thread we've neglected—like a quilt that looks vibrant from afar but unravels up close.

Your devices hum with constant activity—**LinkedIn networks expanding, Instagram reels looping, WhatsApp pings stacking up.** And yet, there's that peculiar hollowness, like standing in a crowded room but feeling **unseen.**

KOLARU & VAATHI ON THE ILLUSION OF CONNECTION

"Everyone's always pretending to connect, but it's all fake," Kolaru muttered, staring gloomily at his buzzing phone. *"Likes, comments, emojis—they mean nothing."*

Vaathi, sitting nearby and sharpening a stick, didn't even glance up. *"True connection isn't about what's on your screen. It's about what's in your silence. When was the last time you sat with someone, said nothing, and still felt understood?"*

Kolaru thought for a moment. *"Does staring at my dog count?"*

"Only if the dog stares back with judgment—like I'm doing now," Vaathi quipped, smirking.

WHY DOES MODERN CONNECTION FEEL SO HOLLOW?

Because we've **traded conversations for captions, shared memes instead of memories,** and **replaced deep interactions with fleeting notifications.** It's quicker, yes. But it's also emptier.

"Alright, wise one," Kolaru said, rolling his eyes. *"Enlighten me. What does real connection look like in this age of hyperconnectivity?"*

Vaathi leaned back, the sharpened stick now forgotten. *"It's like catching a wave. You don't force it. You wait, observe, and align yourself. Connection demands patience, presence, and courage. It's not about paddling furiously."*

"And what if I paddle furiously and drown?" Kolaru asked, half-joking, half-serious.

"Then you learn to swim," Vaathi said matter-of-factly. *"Real connection isn't about avoiding discomfort. It's about embracing it. It's messy. It's vulnerable. But that's where meaning lies."*

THE RAW, CHAOTIC BEAUTY OF CONNECTION

Connection, like life, **isn't meant to be curated**; it's meant to be **chaotic, raw, and real.** In return, it **adds flavor to life, turning the mundane into something extraordinary.**

"So, what if I try and still get wiped out?" Kolaru frowned.

Vaathi shrugged. *"Then you get back on the board and paddle again. But this time, you might notice someone paddling next to you. That's the ride worth taking."*

The interplay between **Kolaru and Vaathi** reflects the **reality of connection—** it's not about **perfection;** it's about **presence.** Relationships come with **unexpected tides, exhilarating rides, and the occasional wipeout.**

Ask Yourself:

- **When someone speaks, do you truly listen?** Or are you just waiting for your turn to talk?
- **When you express empathy, does it go beyond a reflexive "that sucks"?**
- **Does your storytelling connect, or is it just a performance?**

If any of these stings, **you're already on the right path**—because awareness is the first step toward genuine connection. **True connection isn't just about comfort; it's about courage**—the courage to **be present, to listen, and to give more than a polite nod.**

KOLARU & VAATHI ON THE POWER OF SHARED MOMENTS

"Sometimes," Vaathi added, *"it's finding humor in shared absurdities or bonding over unexpected challenges. It's what transforms life's highs into shared celebrations and its lows into bearable burdens. Without connection, even the grandest achievements ring hollow."*

Kolaru nodded slowly, finally grasping the weight of the idea. *"Alright, I'll bite. So how do we do it? How do we connect when everyone's so busy faking it?"*

"Like surfing," Vaathi said. *"You start by listening to the rhythm of the tides. Misunderstandings will ripple, egos will clash, and energies will collide. But if you're willing to adjust your stance and stay present, you'll find the shared rides are smoother—and more fulfilling."*

YOUR MOVE

Life's **greatest joy** and its **deepest challenge** lie not in **riding solo waves** but in **sharing the ocean with others.**

Connection **isn't about ease**—it's about **meaning.**

So, **take a breath, steady your board, and paddle out.** The waves of connection are rolling in, and they hold the power to take you **higher than you ever imagined—together.**

13   TUNING IN – CATCHING THE RHYTHMS OF CONNECTION

Imagine this: you're sitting across from someone, nodding as they speak. But your mind? It's elsewhere—drafting your reply, replaying an argument, or drifting toward tomorrow's tasks. You're hearing their words, but are you truly listening? Are you catching the rhythm of the conversation or merely skating across its surface?

As Kolaru would put it, "I was listening—honestly! I even nodded three times and threw in a 'hmm.' That counts, doesn't it?"

Vaathi, unimpressed, leaned back and said, "Listening isn't about nodding like a bobblehead or saying, 'That's interesting,' while mentally scrolling through your grocery list. True listening creates a bridge, not a checkbox. It demands presence."

Here's the truth: listening isn't hearing. Hearing is passive; listening is intentional. Listening builds connection—a moment of shared understanding. It's as ancient as humanity itself, yet in today's age of hyperconnectivity, it's one we've nearly forgotten.

WHY DOES LISTENING MATTER?

Because connection begins with being heard. True listening fosters trust, dissolves misunderstandings, and nurtures the depth we all crave in relationships. Vaathi's voice echoes here: "Connection is about being heard so deeply that even silence feels like a conversation."

To understand its power, let's look at how listening has shaped humanity:

THE TIMELESS IMPORTANCE OF LISTENING

From prehistoric caves to modern boardrooms, listening has been the foundation of human interaction. Early humans relied on listening for survival—tuning into the rustle of leaves for danger or the crackle of fire for warmth. As civilizations emerged, listening became the bedrock of storytelling, spiritual growth, and leadership.

Figures like Buddha and Marcus Aurelius emphasized listening as a path to wisdom and compassion. Reformers like Martin Luther King Jr. and Nelson Mandela showed that deep listening could reconcile divided communities and inspire lasting change. Even in today's noisy world, listening remains the antidote to misunderstanding and the gateway to connection.

"Yet," Kolaru interjected, "I've sat through people telling their life stories. I listened, and all I got was a headache!"

Vaathi smirked. "That wasn't listening; that was enduring. The difference lies in the intention. Were you truly curious or waiting for your turn to talk?"

WHY LISTENING AND CONFLICT MANAGEMENT GO HAND IN HAND

At its core, listening isn't just about absorbing information; it's about managing the dynamics of a conversation. Conflict often arises not from what is said but from what is not understood.

- Active Listening Prevents Misunderstandings: Most conflicts escalate because people focus on their responses rather than hearing each other. By listening actively, you uncover core issues, not just surface disagreements.

- Empathy Bridges Gaps: Listening with empathy allows you to step into someone else's perspective, dissolving tension and fostering understanding.

- Silence as a Tool: "Sometimes," Vaathi added, "silence is the loudest response. It gives space for clarity, reflection, and connection. The best surfers ride the rhythm of the tide, not their impatience."

Pro Tip: Think of conflict management as surfing choppy waves. The goal isn't to eliminate the turbulence but to ride it skillfully, adapting to the rhythm of the conversation.

PRACTICAL TOOLS TO DEEPEN YOUR LISTENING

"Alright, sensei," Kolaru quipped. "Break it down. How do I stop hearing and start listening?"

Vaathi obliged, gesturing with his ever-present stick:

- **Drop the Distractions:** Silence your devices and focus on the person before you. Presence matters more than perfect words.

- **Ask Open Questions:** Go beyond "How are you?" to "What's been on your mind?" These questions invite meaningful dialog.

- **Mirror Emotions:** Reflect their feelings back to show you're attuned to their experience.

- **Embrace Silences:** Allow pauses to deepen the connection rather than rushing to fill them.

- **Conflict Mapping:** When tension arises, map out the core concerns on both sides. Listening actively can transform arguments into problem-solving sessions.

THE RHYTHM OF CONNECTION

True connection thrives on presence, not perfection. Listening transforms interactions into trust-building bonds, uncovering the gift of meaningful relationships.

"Listening isn't about perfection," Vaathi said. "It's about presence. It's what turns noise into music and words into meaning."

"Or," Kolaru added, "it's what keeps Vaathi from whacking me with that stick every time I interrupt."

Vaathi smirked. "Exactly. Now, let's see if you can ride this wave without wiping out."

Exercise: Tuning Into the Conversation

Take a moment to reflect:

Recall your last meaningful conversation. Did you feel fully present, or were you distracted?

What held you back—stress, your inner monologue, or external devices?

Choose one practical tip from this chapter to apply in your next conversation.

Connection is a rhythm. To tune in, all it takes is presence, curiosity, and the courage to listen deeply. As Kolaru might say, "It's not about catching every word—it's about catching the meaning behind the silence."

14 WAVES OF FORGIVENESS AND VULNERABILITY – RELEASING THE ANCHOR

There's a saying that forgiveness isn't about freeing the other person; it's about freeing yourself. But my teacher once put it even more powerfully: "Forgiving is the empathy we show to ourselves—alarmingly."

At first, it sounded counterintuitive—empathy for ourselves? Alarmingly? But the more I thought about it, the clearer it became. Forgiveness is one of the greatest acts of self-compassion. Yet, it's also one of the hardest.

Why? Because forgiveness demands vulnerability, not just toward others but toward our own pain. It requires us to confront the bitterness, hurt, and anger we carry—sometimes for years. And here's the kicker: the longer we hold onto resentment, the more it becomes an anchor, tethering us to the past and robbing us of the present.

THE WEIGHT WE CARRY

Imagine clinging to a rope tied to a boulder at the edge of a cliff. The weight exhausts you, yet fear keeps you from letting go. Forgiveness is releasing that rope, freeing yourself from resentment's grip. Vulnerability, on the other hand, is stepping forward, exposed, and saying, "This is me." Together, they transform pain into healing and strength.

As Kolaru once lamented to Vaathi, "Why should I forgive someone who hasn't even apologized? Feels like rewarding bad behavior!"

Vaathi, ever patient, replied, "Forgiveness isn't about them, Kolaru. It's about you. Imagine holding a burning coal, waiting to throw it at someone. Who's really getting burned?"

Kolaru frowned. "So you're saying I should just let it go?"

"Letting go doesn't mean excusing their actions," Vaathi said. "It means choosing freedom over bitterness. It's the empathy you show to your future self, so you can live unchained."

WHY FORGIVENESS IS ABOUT YOU

Forgiveness isn't about condoning what happened. It's about acknowledging the pain, learning from it, and deciding that it no longer controls you. When my teacher spoke of forgiveness as an alarming act of self-empathy, it was because of the startling realizations it brings:

- You don't need closure to move on.

- Closure is a myth. Sometimes, the apology you're waiting for will never come, and that's okay. Forgiveness isn't about their words; it's about your peace.

- Resentment feeds the wound.

- Every time you replay the hurt in your mind, you reopen the wound. Forgiveness is the only way to let it scar over and heal.

- You deserve to be free.

- Carrying anger or grudges isn't just emotionally draining; it's physically exhausting. Studies show that forgiveness reduces stress and even improves heart health.

FORGIVENESS MEETS VULNERABILITY

Dr. Brené Brown defines vulnerability as:

"Truth and courage. They're never comfortable, but they're never weakness."

Forgiveness and vulnerability go hand in hand. Forgiveness requires admitting hurt, and vulnerability demands risking exposure. Both are uncomfortable, but they pave the way to healing and deeper connection.

Kolaru, still unconvinced, asked, "But what if I forgive and they hurt me again?"

Vaathi smiled knowingly. "Then you'll know better how to protect your peace next time. Forgiveness doesn't mean opening the door but closing the wound."

STORIES THAT ILLUMINATE FORGIVENESS AND VULNERABILITY

The power of forgiveness and vulnerability has been exemplified throughout history:

1. Jesus on the Cross: "Father, forgive them, for they know not what they do." A profound act of empathy in the face of pain.

2. Draupadi in The Mahabharata: Her vulnerability turned her pain into a rallying cry for justice, transforming suffering into strength.

3. **Kamal Haasan in Anbe Sivam:** Forgiveness transformed scars into empathy, turning personal pain into a universal message of peace.

PRACTICAL TOOLS TO HEAL

Forgiveness and vulnerability may feel overwhelming, but they are skills you can practice:

Forgiveness Practice

1. Acknowledge the Hurt: Write down what happened and how it impacted you.

2. Shift Perspective: Try to empathize with the other person without excusing their actions.

3. Visualize Release: Imagine resentment floating away on a raft, leaving you lighter.

Vulnerability Practice

1. Start Small: Share something personal with someone you trust.

2. Embrace Discomfort: Accept awkwardness as part of growth.

3. Balance with Boundaries: Share intentionally, not excessively.

EXERCISE: RELEASING THE ANCHOR

1. Write down a grudge or fear you've been holding onto. How is it affecting your life?

2. Identify a vulnerable truth you've been afraid to share. How might sharing it set you free?

3. Visualize the freedom you'd feel by letting go. What would it look like to live without this weight?

THE OCEAN WITHIN

Forgiveness clears debris from the shore if the human spirit is an ocean, and vulnerability creates waves that connect. Together, they sustain balance, nurturing growth and authenticity.

Forgiveness isn't easy. It's messy, uncomfortable, and sometimes downright unfair. But when you forgive, you're not just letting someone else off the hook—you're giving yourself permission to heal.

As my teacher said, forgiving is the empathy we show to ourselves—alarming. And in that self-empathy lies the courage to move forward, lighter and freer than before.

Ask Yourself:

*   What weight am I ready to release?
*   What truth am I ready to embrace?

The tides of healing await. Are you ready to ride the waves—lighter, freer, and more alive?

15 STORIES THAT STICK AND COLLABORATION THAT CLICKS

From ancient fireside tales to modern boardroom presentations, storytelling has always been humanity's way of finding meaning in chaos. Collaboration turns these stories into action. Together, they are the ultimate tools for building trust, inspiring action, and creating an unforgettable impact.

But let's face it: expressing yourself isn't always easy. For many, the thought of speaking in a group or stepping onto a stage feels like riding a giant wave without a surfboard. Stage fear and shyness can anchor even the best ideas, leaving them untold.

"Do you ever feel like your heart races just thinking about speaking up?" Kolaru asked, fidgeting nervously. "That's me. Words get stuck, my mind goes blank, and I'm just… frozen."

Vaathi, calm as ever, replied, "Fear of speaking isn't your enemy, Kolaru. It's your untapped energy. The problem isn't the fear; it's thinking you must impress instead of express."

WHY STAGE FEAR AND SHYNESS HOLD US BACK

Stage fright (or glossophobia) and shyness stem from a fear of judgment, failure, or rejection. But here's the truth: these fears don't mean you can't tell great stories or collaborate effectively—they just mean you haven't learned to work with them yet.

- Stage Fear is Energy: The pounding heart, sweaty palms, and racing thoughts are your body's way of preparing you for action. Harnessing that energy can turn fear into focus.

- Shyness is Sensitivity: Shyness often comes from being acutely aware of your environment and how others perceive you. This awareness can be a strength when used to connect authentically.

Pro Tip: Most people don't notice your nerves as much as you think they do. Focus on your message, not their perception.

OVERCOMING STAGE FEAR AND SHYNESS

1. Shift the Focus: Instead of worrying about how you'll be perceived, focus on the value of your message. What are you offering the audience?

2. Prepare and Practice: Rehearse your story or pitch multiple times. Practice in front of a mirror or record yourself to gain confidence.

3. Start Small: Begin by sharing stories in safe, familiar settings, such as with close friends or family. Gradually expand your audience.

4. Embrace Vulnerability: Admitting you're nervous can disarm your fear. Start with, "I'm a little nervous but excited to share this with you."

5. Use Breathing Techniques: Deep, slow breaths calm your nervous system and center your thoughts.

6. Visualize Success: Picture yourself delivering your story confidently and seeing the audience respond positively.

7. Find Your Anchor: Have a phrase, image, or object that reminds you why you're telling your story. This helps ground you in moments of doubt.

OVERCOMING FEAR WITH MODERN TOOLS

For many, stage fright and shyness create a roadblock to storytelling. But modern tools can help turn fear into focus and make even complex stories easy to deliver.

Use Technology to Support Your Story

- Pre-record Critical Sections: If a section of your talk is dense or nerve-wracking, pre-record it. This ensures it's delivered clearly and gives you breathing room during your presentation. It also lets you focus on connecting with the audience rather than stressing over technical details.

- Leverage an iPad/Tablet: Use tools like an iPad with a stylus (projector mode) or a whiteboard to explain concepts live. Writing or drawing while you speak helps anchor the audience's attention and reinforces your message visually.

- Control Your Flow with a Bluetooth PPT Controller: Take charge of your presentation slides with a Bluetooth remote. It keeps you in control, avoids reliance on someone else, and allows you to pace your delivery naturally.

- Incorporate Visual Aids Thoughtfully: Use graphics, diagrams, or short videos to simplify complex points. But don't overdo it—visuals should enhance, not overshadow, your narrative.

- Rehearse Using Tools: Practice with the same tools you'll use during the presentation. Familiarity reduces technical hiccups and nerves.

"Wait, wait," Kolaru interrupted, wide-eyed. "So, I can record a few things and play them during the presentation? Is that even allowed? I didn't know this earlier! No wonder I screwed up so many times—trying to juggle everything on the spot."

Vaathi chuckled. "Of course, it's allowed. The goal isn't to prove you can memorize everything. It's to make sure your message lands. And tools are there to help you, not trip you up."

WHY STORIES MATTER: THE MIND'S OLDEST ALGORITHM

Stories aren't just entertainment—they're survival tools, moral compasses, and emotional bridges. But great storytelling isn't about perfection; it's about connection.

"Remember, Kolaru," Vaathi said, "your story doesn't have to be flawless. It just has to be real."

Here's how storytelling has shaped us:

- Survival Codes: The Mahabharata taught lessons on resilience and strategy.
- Movements: Martin Luther King Jr.'s "I Have a Dream" inspired a nation, while Steve Jobs sold transformation, not just products.

THE NEUROSCIENCE OF STORIES

Stories engage multiple areas of the brain, creating a lasting impact. Facts inform, but stories inspire action because they're tied to emotions.

- A dry fact like, "Sales increased by 20%," is forgettable.
- But "Our team's relentless determination delivered a 20% boost" stays with you.

Pro Tip: The brain doesn't crave perfection; it craves connection.

TOOLS TO OVERCOME FEAR WHILE CRAFTING STORIES

- **Tell to Express, Not Impress:** Your job isn't to dazzle your audience—it's to make them feel something.
- **Start with a Hook:** Grab their attention from the first line. "The winds howled like a thousand wolves" is more gripping than "It was stormy."
- **Use Structure to Your Advantage:** Begin with a hook, present the struggle, and end with resolution. This gives your story clarity and keeps your nerves focused.

- **Find Your Authentic Voice:** Speak as you would to a trusted friend. Avoid over-polished or robotic delivery.

- **Pause and Reflect:** Nervous speakers often rush. Use pauses to emphasize key points and collect your thoughts.

COLLABORATION: WHERE STORIES COME TO LIFE

Storytelling may spark the idea, but collaboration amplifies it into action. From ancient temples to modern tech startups, teamwork transforms stories into tangible achievements.

- Build Psychological Safety: Create an environment where ideas are welcomed without fear of judgment.

  - **Example:** Pixar's Braintrust encourages candid feedback, leading to breakthrough creativity.

- Embrace Conflict: Disagreements, when respectful, drive innovation. Diverse perspectives refine ideas.

- Share the Stage: Collaboration means letting others shine. The best teams are those where credit is shared freely.

EXERCISES TO BUILD CONFIDENCE AND CONNECTION

1. Reframe Your Fear: Write down your thoughts about public speaking or sharing ideas in a group. Replace "I'm going to mess up" with "I'm learning and growing."

2. Practice with a Partner: Share a story with someone you trust. Ask for constructive feedback to boost your confidence.

3. Visualize the Audience as Allies: Imagine the audience as friends rooting for you. This will shift your mindset from "performing" to "connecting."

WRITING YOUR NEXT CHAPTER

"So, Kolaru," Vaathi asked, "what's the first story you're going to tell?"

Kolaru hesitated but then smiled. "Something simple. Something real. And… maybe a little scary. But I think I'm ready."

"Good," Vaathi said. "Every great story starts with a little fear. Just remember—focus on what you want to share, not how you'll be judged."

16 LASTING BONDS – GROWING PEOPLE, CULTIVATING MEANING THROUGH TIDES OF CHANGE

Relationships are the backbone of human experience. They shape our joys, soften our failures, and teach us how to navigate the world. Yet, here's the stark truth: most relationships don't fail from lack of love—they fail from neglect, misunderstanding, and unmet needs.

Modern relationships face unique challenges. With endless digital distractions, we've traded depth for convenience. Conversations are replaced by emojis, conflicts by ghosting, and intimacy by curated Instagram feeds.

As Esther Perel puts it in Mating in Captivity:

> "We expect our partners to be everything—a lover, a best friend, a co-parent, a financial advisor, and a therapist. That's a heavy load for one person."

Mark Manson, in Love Is Not Enough, puts it succinctly:

> "Love is great. Love is necessary. Love is beautiful. But love is not enough."

This chapter delves deep into the art and science of meaningful relationships, blending practical advice, counterintuitive truths, and wisdom from renowned experts.

LOVE IS NOT ENOUGH

Love might bring people together, but it's not enough to keep them together. Relationships need:

- Trust: Built through consistent actions, not occasional grand gestures.

- Respect: Recognizing individuality and maintaining boundaries.

- Effort: Choosing the relationship even when it feels inconvenient.

Mark Manson emphasizes that love alone cannot fix fundamental incompatibilities, broken communication, or lack of effort. It's the foundation, but what you build on it determines its strength.

Pro Tip: Gary Chapman explains in The 5 Love Languages that people express and receive love differently. If you're speaking in mismatched "languages", no amount of love will feel like enough. Identify your love language and your partner's—whether it's quality time, acts of service, or physical touch—and act on it intentionally.

BOUNDARIES ARE BRIDGES, NOT WALLS

One of the most misunderstood aspects of relationships is boundaries. People often see them as barriers, but in reality, boundaries protect relationships by creating respect and clarity.

Mark Manson's Wisdom: "Boundaries mean taking responsibility for your own actions and emotions, while NOT taking responsibility for the actions and emotions of others."

HOW TO SET HEALTHY BOUNDARIES:

- Communicate Early: Don't wait for resentment to build before addressing limits.

- Be Clear, Not Defensive: Instead of saying, "You're too demanding," say, "I need time to recharge so I can show up better."

- Stay Consistent: Respect your own boundaries to encourage others to do the same.

Vaathi's insight: "Boundaries don't push people away; they show them where they're welcome to meet you."

COMMUNICATION IS THE LIFEBLOOD OF CONNECTION

Every relationship guide will tell you communication is key, but let's simplify what that actually means:

THE 3 PILLARS OF COMMUNICATION:

1. Listening to Understand: Don't listen to reply; listen to hear.
2. **Pro Tip:** Repeat back what you've heard to show understanding: "So, what you're saying is…"
3. Clarity Over Assumption: Say what you mean instead of expecting others to read your mind.
4. Consistency in Small Acts: Frequent check-ins maintain connection, even when life gets busy.

CONFLICT ISN'T THE PROBLEM—AVOIDANCE IS

Many believe avoiding arguments is the secret to happy relationships. But the truth is that healthy conflict builds stronger bonds.

Healthy Conflict Techniques:

"Yes, and" Approach: Validate their perspective before adding your own.

"Yes, I see why you're upset, and I think we can work on this together."

Focus on Solutions, Not Blame: Instead of "You always make us late," say, "How can we manage time better next time?"

- Take Pauses: Heated moments often escalate unnecessarily. A pause can prevent saying something you regret.
- Mark Manson's **Insight:** "The point of conflict in a relationship is not to 'win'—it's to understand."

RELATIONSHIPS ARE ECOSYSTEMS, NOT CHECKLISTS

Lasting relationships aren't about ticking boxes like "date nights" or "anniversaries celebrated." They thrive when treated like ecosystems—dynamic, interdependent, and constantly evolving.

- Celebrate Growth: Your partner isn't static; they'll grow and change. Celebrate their evolution instead of resisting it.

- Respect Individuality: Independence isn't a threat to connection; it's a strength.

- Express Gratitude: Regular appreciation fosters positivity and resilience during tough times.

As John Gottman suggests in The Seven Principles for Making Marriage Work, even simple acts like saying "thank you" or "I appreciate you" can repair cracks in the foundation.

PRACTICAL TOOLS FOR THRIVING RELATIONSHIPS

1. The Feedback Loop: Ask regularly, "What's one thing I can do to make us better?"

2. Active Gratitude Practice: Write down one thing you appreciate about another person daily.

3. Celebrate Micro-Moments: Don't wait for grand occasions. Celebrate the little things—a shared laugh, a kind gesture, a solved problem.

4. Conflict Mapping: When tensions rise, map out the issue together. Identify what you're both feeling, what triggered it, and what the resolution might look like.

THE HARSH TRUTH

Here's the reality no one wants to admit: relationships don't fail overnight. They fail because we stop showing up in the small, unremarkable moments. We stop listening. We stop trying. We assume the other person will always be there, no matter how little effort we put in.

As Sue Johnson explains in Hold Me Tight, emotional disconnect, not lack of love, is what breaks people apart. Repairing that connection means showing up consistently, even when it's uncomfortable.

Kolaru's Question

One quiet evening, after reflecting on it all, Kolaru asked, "Vaathi, has anyone ever truly become an expert in relationships? It feels like the more advice we get, the messier things become."

Vaathi chuckled. "No one, Kolaru. That's why there are thousands of books, websites, and coaches on this topic. The truth is that the more you try to control relationships, the more unpredictable they get.

"You don't master relationships; you learn to surf them. Balance, patience, and adaptability—that's the real secret."

ASK YOURSELF:

- What's one small act of care you can do for someone today?
- How can you approach conflict with more empathy?
- What assumptions about relationships might you need to let go of?

Relationships are like waves; they're unpredictable and require effort to ride. But with the right mindset, they'll carry you farther than you ever imagined. Grab your board, find your balance, and start surfing.

THE NEGOTIATION SYMPHONY – MASTERING BALANCE, PERSUASION, AND IMPACT

Negotiation is often seen as a battlefield of offers, counteroffers, and power plays. But in truth, it's a dance of strategy, psychology, and empathy. It's not about dominating the other party but about creating win-win outcomes where everyone feels valued and respected.

"Negotiation is like surfing," Vaathi said. "It's not about overpowering the wave; it's about riding it skillfully and knowing when to push or let go."

This chapter explores how to approach negotiation as an art form, blending authenticity, emotional intelligence, and strategic thinking to achieve impactful outcomes that last beyond the deal.

PREPARATION – KNOW YOUR WAVE BEFORE YOU PADDLE IN

Preparation is where great negotiations are won or lost. Before you step into any discussion, you need clarity about your goals and a deep understanding of the other party's priorities.

- Clarity is Key: Define your goals, bottom line (non-negotiables), and areas of flexibility.

- ○ **Pro Tip:** Use the BATNA Framework (Best Alternative to a Negotiated Agreement) to avoid making decisions out of desperation.

- Empathy as Your Compass: Understand the other party's motivations, fears, and desired outcomes. This isn't about manipulation but tailoring your approach to align with their needs.

- Questions to ask yourself: What does success look like for them? What challenges are they trying to solve?

  - ○ **Example:** If a supplier prioritizes reliability over cost, frame your proposal around consistent delivery rather than price savings.

PLAY THE PERSON, NOT THE GAME

In negotiation, people make decisions—not robots. The more you understand the person across the table, the more effectively you can collaborate.

- Avoid Ultimatums: Ultimatums corner the other party, fostering defensiveness and resistance.

- Reframe: Instead of: "This is my final offer." Say: "Here's how we can make this work for both of us."

- Leverage Cognitive Biases: Anchoring Effect: Set the tone with the first offer to establish a strong baseline.
  - ○ **Example:** In salary discussions, starting at £90,000 shifts the negotiation anchor upward.

- Loss Aversion: Highlight the risks of walking away to motivate agreement.
  - ○ **Example:** "This deal secures long-term stability in a volatile market."

- Reciprocity Principle: Small acts of goodwill encourage reciprocation.
  - ○ **Example:** "We've prepared a draft to simplify the process for you."

CONTROL THE NARRATIVE – MASTER THE FRAME

How you frame your conversation can shift the entire tone of the negotiation. Instead of focusing on concessions, focus on collaboration.

- Reframe the Conversation: Instead of asking, "Can we lower the price?" ask, "How can we build a long-term partnership that benefits us both?"

- Use the "Yes, and" Strategy: Acknowledge their concerns and build collaboratively:

"Yes, I see your point, and that's why this solution addresses both our needs."

NAVIGATING CONFLICT – FINDING COMMON WAVES

Conflict in negotiation isn't a setback but an opportunity to align divergent perspectives.

- Steps to Resolution: Focus on the Problem, Not the Person: Replace "You're being unreasonable." with "Let's clarify where our goals differ."

- Acknowledge Concerns: Validate their perspective before presenting yours.

- Reiterate Shared Goals: **For example,** "We both want this project to succeed—how can we achieve that together?"

- Silence as a Tool: Strategic pauses often compel the other party to fill the gap, revealing deeper priorities and insights.

BUILDING RAPPORT – THE FOUNDATION OF TRUST

Negotiation isn't just about terms but about relationships; trust is the glue that holds deals together.

- Techniques to Build Connection: Start with Shared Goals: "We both want this partnership to succeed."

- **Use Humor:** A lighthearted comment can diffuse tension and reset the atmosphere.

- **Acknowledge Strengths:** Compliment their expertise or approach to create goodwill.

- **Historical Example:** Nelson Mandela built rapport with prison guards during his imprisonment, transforming adversaries into allies. This was instrumental in South Africa's eventual reconciliation.

PRACTICE MAKES PROGRESS – EXERCISES FOR MASTERY

- **Empathy Mapping:** Write down what the other party is likely thinking, feeling, saying, and doing. Use this map to tailor your approach.

- **Silent Pause Challenge:** Pause for three seconds after making a key point. Note how the other party responds.

- Role-Playing Scenarios: Practice with a partner, alternating roles as negotiator and opposition. This builds adaptability and sharpens techniques.

NEGOTIATION ARCHETYPES – KNOW YOUR STYLE

Understanding your negotiation style helps you play to your strengths and adapt to others.

- **The Analyst: Strength:** Data-driven and logical. **Strategy:** Present clear evidence and rational arguments.

- **The Empath: Strength**: Values trust and relationships. **Strategy:** Build rapport and align with shared values.

- **The Visionary: Strength:** Focused on long-term goals. **Strategy:** Show how your proposal supports their broader vision.

NAVIGATION, NOT DOMINATION

Negotiation isn't about winning; it's about collaboration. As Mark Manson emphasizes in Models, authenticity and vulnerability create genuine connections. The same principles apply here.

Pro Tip: Frame offers as mutual gains. People remember how you made them feel, not just the deal's terms.

KEY TAKEAWAYS

- **Avoid Ultimatums:** They escalate tension instead of fostering collaboration.

- **Empathy Wins:** Understand their motivations and align your offer accordingly.

- **Silence Speaks Volumes:** Strategic pauses reveal deeper insights.

- **Build Bridges, Not Barriers:** Negotiation is about relationships, not domination.

- **Crafting Your Symphony:** Negotiation is an intricate symphony of logic, emotion, and strategy. The best negotiators, like skilled surfers, know when to push, pause, or let the wave carry them.

"Vaathi," Kolaru asked, "do you think negotiation is really about winning?"

"No, Kolaru," Vaathi said, smiling. "It's about harmony. It's about making sure everyone leaves the table feeling heard, valued, and respected. That's the real victory."

REFLECTION:

What's your next negotiation?

How will you harmonize strategy, psychology, and empathy to craft your symphony?

Ride the wave and create connections that resonate long after the deal is done.

18

HARMONY IN DUALITY – WHEN INTROVERT MEETS EXTROVERT

Every individual carries within them a blend of introversion and extroversion—a dynamic spectrum rather than a fixed identity. Introverts draw strength from introspection, solitude, and depth, while extroverts thrive on energy, connection, and spontaneity.

These traits aren't opposites; they're complementary forces. When balanced, they create relationships and teams capable of profound creativity, resilience, and growth.

One evening, as they debated personalities over chai, Kolaru asked, "So, what happens when an introvert and extrovert are stuck working together? Chaos?"

Vaathi smirked. "Not chaos, Kolaru. It's like mixing calm waters with strong tides—you get waves that move forward with depth and energy. The secret lies in understanding how to navigate the currents together."

THE INTROVERT AND EXTROVERT WITHIN

Introverts: Calm Lagoons of Quiet Strength: Contrary to stereotypes, introversion isn't shyness but a preference for introspection and depth.

Strengths:

- Keen Observation: They notice details others might miss.

- Deep Empathy: Active listening fosters meaningful connections.
- Focused Problem-Solving: Time alone sparks creative breakthroughs.

Challenges:

- Struggling in high-energy, fast-paced environments.
- Hesitation to express ideas in larger groups.

Pro Tip: Recharge before social engagements with journaling, mindfulness, or quiet reflection.

Example: J.K. Rowling's introspective nature led to the creation of the Harry Potter universe during long train rides, proving that solitude can spark unparalleled creativity.

Extroverts: Energetic Waves of Enthusiasm: Extroverts thrive on dynamic interactions, leading through charisma and inspiring action.

Strengths:

- Energizing Teams: Their enthusiasm motivates those around them.
- Broad Networking: They excel at building diverse connections.
- Spontaneous Collaboration: Brainstorming and quick decisions come naturally.

Challenges:

- Over-reliance on external validation.
- Difficulty pausing for introspection.

Pro Tip: Channel energy strategically for high-stakes moments, followed by downtime to recharge.

Example: Steve Jobs's extroverted flair turned Apple product launches into global events, showcasing the magnetic power of charisma.

NAVIGATING THE SPECTRUM IN RELATIONSHIPS

Whether at work, at home, or among friends, blending introversion and extroversion requires awareness and adaptability.

With Mentors: Learn and Reflect - Combine introverted humility with extroverted curiosity.

Tip: Ask open-ended questions to gain deeper insights.

Example: Oprah Winfrey's relationship with Maya Angelou was built on mutual respect, as Oprah's extroverted curiosity paired beautifully with Maya's wisdom and depth.

With Beginners: Guide and Inspire: Patience and relatability bridge gaps in experience.

Tip: Use clear, relatable examples to simplify concepts.

Example: Bill Gates explains complex ideas in accessible ways, inspiring budding innovators without overwhelming them.

Across the Spectrum: Build Bridges: Adapt to others' energy levels to foster collaboration.

Tip: Extroverts can tone down enthusiasm, while introverts can step up in group settings.

Example: Barack Obama balanced introspective decision-making with extroverted public speaking, seamlessly connecting with diverse audiences.

THE PSYCHOLOGY OF DUALITY

The Dopamine Connection: Extroverts are energized by dopamine, thriving on external stimuli, while introverts may feel overstimulated in high-energy settings.

Tip: Introverts in overstimulating environments can take short breaks to reset.

The Role of the Amygdala: Introverts process stimuli more deeply, leading to over-analysis and decision delays.

Exercise: Reflect on a decision where the timing was off and strategize how to improve future responses.

LEVERAGING DUALITY FOR SUCCESS

The Power of Opposites: Introverts and extroverts bring complementary strengths to the table.

Example: Susan Cain's introspection (Quiet) and Tony Robbins' extroverted energy (Awaken the Giant Within) illustrate how these seemingly opposite traits can create a transformative impact.

CONNECTION IN DIVERSE ENVIRONMENTS

Cross-Spectrum Innovation: Teams thrive when introverts' insights and extroverts' energy unite.

Tip: Balance loud and quieter voices to ensure all ideas are heard.

Example: Pixar fosters innovation by blending introverted observation with extroverted collaboration, encouraging diverse perspectives.

EXERCISES FOR SELF-AWARENESS AND GROWTH

1. The Energy Journal: Track your interactions for a week, noting when you felt energized (extroversion) or drained (introversion). Use these insights to balance your engagements.

2. The Silence and Speech Test: **Extroverts:** Practice active listening without interrupting. Introverts: Commit to sharing one unique insight in your next group setting.

REAL-LIFE STORIES OF BALANCE

- Jacinda Ardern: Combined introverted empathy with decisive extroverted action during the Christchurch shooting, exemplifying balanced leadership.

- Susan Cain: Overcame her introversion to deliver a TED Talk that resonated globally, staying true to her reflective nature.

- Barack Obama: Mastered public charisma while relying on introspection for thoughtful decision-making.

THE SWEET SPOT – DUALITY IN HARMONY

The secret to thriving relationships and teams isn't forcing everyone into one mold but embracing the spectrum of personalities.

Respect Differences, Celebrate **Strengths:**

- Introverts thrive on solitude and meaningful connections.
- Extroverts bring energy and spontaneity. Together, they create balance.

Pro Tip: Harmony emerges from understanding, not from trying to make one personality dominate the other.

NAVIGATING THE OCEAN OF CONNECTION

Like the tides, personalities ebb and flow. By embracing introversion and extroversion as complementary forces, we foster trust, innovation, and resilience in relationships.

Kolaru's **Reflection:**

"So, you're saying I don't need to change who I am to fit in?" Kolaru asked, tilting his head.

"Exactly," Vaathi replied. "Introvert or extrovert, it's not about being someone else. It's about knowing when to reflect when to act, and when to let the waves carry you forward.

LEADERSHIP REDEFINED

(BABYSITTING GROWN-UPS, BUT MAKE IT COOL)

Leadership isn't about titles, corner offices, or wielding authority through fear. It's about embracing chaos and channeling it into purpose. Forget the Instagram-perfect version of leadership—polished speeches and motivational memes. Real leadership is messy, uncomfortable, and often feels like juggling flaming torches in a storm.

"Leadership is like surfing," Vaathi said. "It's not about overpowering the wave; it's about riding it skillfully and knowing when to push or let go."

This part is your chance to explore leadership beyond the clichés. It's not about being the loudest voice in the room or having all the answers. It's about showing up, staying authentic, and leading with courage—whether managing a team, guiding a family, or simply trying to lead yourself.

ARE YOU A LEADER—OR JUST A MANAGER?

Before we dive in, ask yourself:

- Do people follow you because they trust you—or because they fear you?

- When things go wrong, do you take responsibility—or pass the blame?

- Are you inspiring action—or micromanaging every detail?

If these questions make you uncomfortable, good. Leadership isn't about comfort; it's about growth.

WHO'S LEADING YOU?

Here's the kicker: leadership doesn't start with managing others. It begins with managing yourself. You can't lead others to clarity, purpose, or resilience if you're struggling with your own chaos.

But let's face it—most of us aren't born leaders. We start as Kolaru, stumbling through life, dodging responsibility, and learning everything the hard way. And if you think you've already "made it," ask yourself this:

- Are you truly leading—or just surviving?

- Do you have a clear vision—or are you winging it day by day?

The good news? Even the greatest leaders were once Kolarus. The difference is that they had a Vaathi—a guide, mentor, or even a harsh reality check that pushed them to evolve.

LEADERSHIP IS A BALANCING ACT

Can you balance confidence with humility? Influence without authority? Strength with vulnerability? These aren't just nice-to-have qualities—they're critical survival skills in today's hyper-connected, ever-changing world.

And here's where it gets real:

- Do you know how to handle people who act like toddlers in a corporate setting?

- Can you inspire a vision without sounding like a walking Hallmark card?

- Do you know when to step up and when to step back?

QUESTIONS TO KEEP YOU THINKING

Over the next six chapters, we'll dive into the heart of leadership—its messy realities, tough choices, and incredible rewards. But before we begin, let's set the stage with a few questions to keep in mind:

- What's your leadership style—and is it working for you?

- Do you create space for others to grow—or are you the bottleneck?

- When was the last time you led by example, even when no one was watching?

"Leadership sounds like babysitting grown-ups who act like kids," Kolaru grumbled.

"Sometimes it is," Vaathi replied. "But your job isn't to coddle them but to guide them. To challenge them. To create the conditions where they can thrive."

"Leadership isn't about being the hero," Vaathi said. "It's about building a team of heroes and knowing when to step out of the spotlight."

READY TO REDEFINE LEADERSHIP?

This part isn't just for managers or CEOs—it's for parents, students, entrepreneurs, or anyone navigating moments of leadership in life. Leadership isn't about perfection; it's about showing up.

So, are you ready to lead—not with authority, but with authenticity? Let's dive into the storm and learn how to ride the waves of leadership with purpose, clarity, and, yes, a little swagger.

19 LEADING WITH CONFIDENCE – FROM SURFER TO GUIDE

Leadership isn't glamorous: It's messy, unpredictable, and often feels like babysitting grown-ups. Adults are just kids with bigger vocabularies and more elaborate excuses. As a leader, your job isn't to control their chaos but to guide their brilliance, manage the mess, and somehow keep your sanity intact.

"Leadership is like herding cats in a thunderstorm," Kolaru muttered.

"And yet," Vaathi replied, "the best leaders don't chase the cats. They guide them with confidence, clarity, and a sense of humor."

This chapter isn't about chasing the illusion of the "perfect leader". It's about embracing authenticity, humor, and empathy while turning leadership chaos into a symphony of progress.

THE SURFBOARD OF CONFIDENCE: WHY LEADERSHIP STARTS WITH YOU

Your confidence—or lack of it—sets the tone for your team. If you lead with composure and conviction, they'll feel empowered. If you're erratic or indecisive, the waves of uncertainty ripple through everyone.

"A ship in harbor is safe, but that's not what ships are built for." – John A. Shedd

But here's the thing: confidence without compassion turns into arrogance. The best leaders inspire not through intimidation but through kindness and consistency.

Example: Jacinda Ardern, during the Christchurch tragedy, led with both empathy and decisiveness, inspiring trust and unity when it was needed most.

LEADING WITH HEART AND HUMOR

"Leadership without humor," Vaathi said, "is like surfing without waves—flat and forgettable."

Humor is a secret weapon. It builds camaraderie, defuses tension, and reminds your team that even during challenges, joy matters.

Pro Tip: Use humor to connect, not to condescend. Self-deprecating humor works wonders—it humanizes you without undermining your authority.

LISTEN FIRST, ACT SECOND

"People follow leaders who listen," Vaathi said. "Not the ones who just bark orders."

Great leadership is about building partnerships through listening. When your team feels heard, they're more likely to trust your decisions—even the tough ones.

Example: Satya Nadella transformed Microsoft's culture by listening deeply to employees, fostering collaboration, and aligning the company's vision with its people.

Pro Tip: During one-on-one meetings, ask open-ended questions like:

- "What challenges are you facing right now?"
- "How can I support you better?"

LEADERSHIP IN ACTION: LEARN FROM YOUR TEAM

"Every leader learns twice," Vaathi said. "Once from their own experience, and once from their team's."

- Know Their **Strengths:** The best leaders identify unique abilities and assign challenges that align with individual talents.

Example: The Wright brothers balanced meticulous planning with bold experimentation, creating a partnership that soared.

- Own Your Wipeouts: Admitting mistakes doesn't weaken your authority—it strengthens trust.

Caveat: Be honest, but don't overshare. Saying, "I miscalculated that timeline," builds trust. Saying, "I have no idea what I'm doing," undermines it.

- Build Trust: Align your words with actions. Keep promises, give credit where it's due, and be consistent.

Pro Tip: Celebrate your team's success publicly and offer constructive feedback privately.

DECISION-MAKING: SET THE TONE

"Indecision is worse than a bad decision," Vaathi said. "Because it leaves everyone floundering."

Clear decisions inspire confidence—even if they're not perfect. Hesitation breeds confusion, while decisiveness fosters trust.

Example: Elon Musk's bold calls during Tesla's early struggles inspired trust, not because they were risk-free, but because they were clear and well-communicated.

Pro Tip: Before making a decision, ask yourself:

1. Does this align with the team's goals?

2. What are the risks of waiting?

3. Act swiftly and refine as needed.

CELEBRATE THE WAVES THEY RIDE

Small wins build momentum. Recognize achievements, even the small ones—whether it's meeting a tough deadline or simply surviving a stressful week.

Example: Pixar's "Braintrust" meetings celebrate creativity while offering constructive critique, fostering a culture of innovation and trust.

ENCOURAGE GROWTH: PUSH THEM TO SURF BIGGER WAVES

"A great leader," Vaathi said, "sees potential where others see limitations."

Encourage your team to step outside their comfort zones. That's where real growth happens.

- **Pro Tip:** Pair seasoned team members with juniors for mutual learning. Mentors gain fresh perspectives, and mentees build confidence.

CREATE WAVES FOR OTHERS TO RIDE

Leadership isn't about being the best surfer. It's about creating opportunities for others to shine.

Pro Tip: Regularly ask for feedback on your leadership.

1. Identify one area for improvement (e.g. delegating better).
2. Act on the feedback and measure the impact.

QUOTE TO REMEMBER

"Leadership is about making others better as a result of your presence and making sure that impact lasts in your absence." – Sheryl Sandberg

LEADERSHIP ISN'T A DESTINATION

Leadership isn't about perfection; it's about showing up with authenticity, empathy, and humor, learning along the way, and inspiring others to create waves of their own.

So, grab your surfboard, steady your footing, and guide your crew to greatness.

20   Breaking Rules Like a Pro – The Art of Disruption

Breaking the rules isn't about reckless rebellion but about purposeful evolution. True disruption tears down what doesn't work and builds something transformative. It's like riding a rogue wave that reshapes the shoreline, leaving behind a world of new possibilities.

"Change without disruption is just aging," Vaathi remarked, sharpening his metaphorical stick. "Real progress comes when you're bold enough to break what's holding you back."

Kolaru, ever the skeptic, smirked. "And when that backfires?"

"That's the beauty of it," Vaathi said. "You learn to ride the waves, not fight them."

This chapter is your guide to responsible rule-breaking—how to innovate with precision, navigate resistance, and ensure your disruptions lead to progress, not chaos.

RULE-BREAKING WITH PURPOSE: A BALANCING ACT

Not All Rules Are Created Equal: Some rules protect us; others stifle us. The first step in disruption is identifying which rules to break.

Pro Tip: Break rules that hinder progress, not those that preserve trust.

Example: Netflix disrupted Blockbuster by eliminating late fees, introducing streaming, and personalizing content. They didn't destroy entertainment—they redefined it.

Reflection: Ask yourself: Is this rule hindering growth or efficiency? How could breaking it create value?

KNOW THE WAVES BEFORE YOU RIDE THEM

"Breaking a rule without understanding its purpose," Vaathi warned, "is recklessness. Disruption, like surfing, requires knowing the waters before you dive in."

Pro Tip: Start small—test the waters before attempting a tidal wave of change.

Example: Elon Musk didn't disrupt the auto industry overnight. Tesla began with luxury electric cars, proving the viability of sustainable transport step by step.

BREAKING RULES, NOT TRUST

Disruption often invites resistance because people fear uncertainty more than change. Clear communication and a shared vision are your antidotes.

Example: Satya Nadella transformed Microsoft's rigid culture by championing a "growth mindset." By explaining his vision transparently, he earned trust before challenging norms.

Insight: Disrupt without alienating—explain how the change benefits everyone.

LESSONS FROM THE FOXES OF YELLOWSTONE

"Disruption doesn't mean destruction," Vaathi said. "It's about creating ripple effects that lead to balance."

When foxes were reintroduced to Yellowstone, they stabilized the ecosystem without wreaking havoc.

Key Insight: Find your "fox"—a small, purposeful change that drives systemic progress.

THE TOOLS OF DISRUPTION: CURIOSITY, COURAGE, AND EMPATHY

Great disruptors don't just break rules, they reimagine them.

- **Curiosity:** Ask, "What if?" Steve Jobs asked, "What if a phone could also be a music player and a browser?" The result: the iPhone.
- **Courage:** Embrace failure as part of the process. How do you handle setbacks?
- **Empathy:** Understand how change affects others. Airbnb empathized with travelers seeking affordable, personalized stays, disrupting hospitality.

THE ETHICS OF RULE-BREAKING

"Disruption without ethics is exploitation," Vaathi said. "A true disruptor uplifts rather than exploits."

Example: Uber revolutionized transportation but faced backlash for labor practices. Ethical disruptors prioritize long-term benefits for all stakeholders.

Caveat: Always weigh the ripple effects. Are you creating progress or harm?

NAVIGATING RESISTANCE: INVOLVE YOUR CREW

"People fear change they don't understand," Vaathi explained. "Bring them into the process."

Pro Tip: Frame disruption as an opportunity, not a threat.

Example: Apple doesn't just launch products; they tell stories, ensuring their audience feels part of the journey.

CREATIVITY IN BROKEN NORMS

History's greatest innovations came from challenging conventions:

- Albert Einstein: Redefined physics by questioning Newtonian principles.
- Pablo Picasso: Revolutionized art with Cubism.

Insight: Creativity thrives in disruption, but only when it's rooted in purpose.

Caveat: Not all rules are meant to be broken—choose wisely.

FOLLOW-THROUGH: MAKING DISRUPTION STICK

Disruption without execution is just noise. To make it last:

1. Communicate clearly to reduce fear.
2. Engage stakeholders early.
3. Equip others with tools to adapt.
4. Gather feedback regularly to refine your approach.

Pro Tip: Frame your disruption as a story—people connect with narratives, not directives.

THE DISRUPTOR'S MANIFESTO

Breaking rules isn't rebellion but a responsibility. Great disruptors balance boldness with strategy, confidence with empathy, and progress with ethics.

Before breaking a rule, ask yourself:

- Why am I breaking this rule?
- Will it create progress or chaos?

Pro Tip: Disruption is like surfing—you ride the waves but never break the board.

CLOSING QUOTE

"Disruption isn't about destroying the past. It's about creating a future where everyone thrives."

Ready to disrupt? Choose your wave, steady your footing, and reshape the shoreline with purpose.

21

EMPOWERING OTHERS – SHARING THE SPOTLIGHT, SHARING THE LOAD

Imagine trying to surf every wave in the ocean by yourself. Exhausting, right? Leadership without delegation is just that—an impossible solo act. Great leaders don't hog the waves; they assemble a team of world-class surfers and let them shine.

Leadership isn't about individual heroics. It's about riding waves as a team where humility and delegation are your two most underrated superpowers. Master these, and you'll not only lighten your load but also foster collaboration, trust, and innovation. Bonus? You finally get to enjoy your coffee while it's still hot.

"Vaathi," Kolaru grumbled, slouching in his chair. "Why do leaders always tell us to 'take initiative' but then never let go of control?"

Vaathi smirked, stirring his coffee with deliberate calm. "Because they're not real leaders yet, Kolaru. A true leader trusts their team. And trust, like surfing a perfect wave, is built one paddle at a time."

Kolaru raised an eyebrow. "So, all this talk about 'teamwork'—it's just leaders passing their problems down the chain?"

"No," Vaathi said, leaning forward. "It's about sharing the load, not dumping it. Real leaders create leaders, not followers."

HUMILITY: THE QUIET POWER OF GREAT LEADERS

Contrary to popular belief, humility isn't a weakness—it's a superpower.

"Look, Kolaru," Vaathi began, "humble leaders don't act like they're the smartest person in the room. They know the smartest room is one where everyone's ideas are heard. Humility isn't about stepping down; it's about stepping aside to let others rise."

"Stepping aside sounds like a fancy way of avoiding responsibility," Kolaru quipped.

"Wrong again," Vaathi replied. "Humble leaders do the hard work—listening, trusting, and celebrating others' wins. It's how you build teams that thrive."

WHY HUMILITY WORKS

1. Builds Trust: Admitting you don't have all the answers creates openness.

2. (Spoiler alert: Nobody thought you were omniscient anyway.)

3. Fosters Collaboration: Humble leaders crowdsource brilliance instead of hoarding mediocrity.

4. Inspires Loyalty: Teams follow leaders who prioritize the mission over their egos.

Example: In 2014, Elon Musk opened Tesla's patents to competitors. It wasn't about surrendering dominance but advancing a vision bigger than himself.

"See? Humility isn't just nice—it's effective," Vaathi said. "Focus on the mission, not the applause."

DELEGATION: THE ART OF LETTING GO WITHOUT LOSING CONTROL

Delegation isn't about dumping work but about empowering others to grow.

"Alright, Vaathi," Kolaru said, "but what if I delegate and people mess up? Then I look bad!"

"That's your problem, Kolaru," Vaathi replied, smiling knowingly. "You're so worried about looking bad that you don't realize delegation is about letting others shine."

THE DELEGATION FORMULA

Know What to Let Go: Focus on what only you can do; delegate the rest. **Example:** Sundar Pichai empowers his teams to lead, freeing him to focus on strategy.

Match People to Tasks: Assign work based on individual strengths and aspirations.

Example: Richard Branson encourages employees to innovate independently while providing them with the tools for success.

Communicate Clearly: Ambiguity is the enemy of delegation. Provide clear instructions and align on goals.

"Micromanaging isn't leadership—it's babysitting," Vaathi added. "Find the balance between oversight and trust."

ADMITTING MISTAKES: A SIGN OF STRENGTH

"Mistakes, Kolaru," Vaathi said, "aren't failures—they're lessons in disguise. Admitting them doesn't weaken your authority; it strengthens trust."

"So, you're saying I should just announce every screw-up?" Kolaru asked.

"No, not every screw-up," Vaathi clarified, laughing. "Admit when it matters. 'I miscalculated the timeline, but here's how we'll fix it' builds credibility. Saying, 'I have no idea what I'm doing,' doesn't."

Pro Tip: Frame mistakes as growth opportunities. Share what went wrong, what you learned, and how you'll improve.

LESSONS FROM LEADERS WHO EMPOWERED OTHERS

The greatest leaders built success on humility and delegation:

- Satya Nadella: Revitalized Microsoft with empathy-driven leadership.

- Richard Branson: "Train people well enough so they can leave, but treat them well enough so they don't want to."

- Nelson Mandela: Led from behind, giving others the spotlight while steering the mission forward.

"See, Kolaru?" Vaathi said. "Leadership isn't about holding the spotlight. It's about sharing it."

EXERCISES TO STRENGTHEN EMPOWERMENT

- Delegation Dare: Identify one task you're holding onto unnecessarily. Delegate it this week and reflect on the outcome.

- Ego Audit: Ask for anonymous feedback on your leadership style. Choose one suggestion to implement.

- Delegation Matrix: Categorize tasks:

  - Retain: Tasks only you can do.

  - Delegate Now: Tasks others can handle immediately.

  - Prepare to Delegate: Tasks you can groom others for.

THE RIPPLE EFFECT OF EMPOWERMENT

When you delegate with purpose and humility, you inspire growth and create a ripple effect. Individual efforts turn into collective triumphs.

"Leadership isn't solo surfing, Kolaru; it's riding waves together," Vaathi said. "Empower your team, and you'll all go farther than you ever imagined."

"Remember, Kolaru," Vaathi concluded, "the strongest leaders are the ones who make others stronger."

"It is better to lead from behind and to put others in front, especially when you celebrate victory. You take the front line when there is danger. Then people will appreciate your leadership." Nelson Mandela

22 LEARNING FROM LEGENDS – LESSONS FROM THEIR TRIUMPHS AND MISTAKES

WHAT MAKES A LEGEND?

Is it their dazzling success, unyielding perseverance, or the wisdom they gain from spectacular wipeouts? Spoiler: it's all three, blended with impeccable timing and a dash of luck. While we celebrate icons for their triumphs, their stumbles often hold the richest lessons.

As Rocky Balboa famously said, "It ain't about how hard you hit. It's about how hard you can get hit and keep moving forward." Legends aren't flawless; they turn scars into maps, leading others to greatness.

This chapter delves into the habits, triumphs, and failures of iconic leaders, helping you shape your style. Think of it as "borrowing their cheat codes" to success—without violating copyright laws.

"Vaathi," Kolaru said, flipping through his phone, "everyone's obsessed with success stories. But why don't people talk about their screw-ups?"

Vaathi leaned back and smirked. "Because success feels good, Kolaru, but failure is where the real lessons hide. Legends aren't made from applause; they're made from comebacks."

THE CASE FOR BORROWING BRILLIANCE

"Legends aren't born—they're built," Vaathi continued, "through experience, collaboration, and risks. Even the greatest borrowed brilliance from others."

Examples?

- Steve Jobs found inspiration in calligraphy and Zen minimalism.
- Oprah Winfrey turned personal pain into a purpose-driven empire.
- Elon Musk transformed failure into rocket fuel.

"Here's the trick, Kolaru," Vaathi added. "Borrow brilliance, but make it your own. Success leaves clues—and bloopers. Study both."

LESSON 1: STAND ON THE SHOULDERS OF GIANTS

"Success lights the way, but failure teaches you where the potholes are," Vaathi explained.

Examples of Borrowing Brilliance:

- Elon Musk: Three failed SpaceX launches almost bankrupted him, but he used the lessons to revolutionize space travel.
- Oprah Winfrey: Learned empathy and authenticity from her mentors but created her own voice to transform media.

Pro Tip: Don't be seduced by highlight reels. Always ask, "What's the story behind the story?"

LESSON 2: FAILURE IS THE ULTIMATE TEACHER

"Failure isn't the end of the road—it's the universe yelling, 'Try again, but smarter,'" Vaathi said, pointing his coffee cup at Kolaru for emphasis.

Examples of Failure as Feedback:

- Kodak: They invented digital photography but clung to film, becoming a cautionary tale.
- Blockbuster: Dismissed Netflix, only to be buried by streaming culture.

"Let me guess," Kolaru interrupted, "you're about to say failure builds character?"

Vaathi grinned. "It does if you listen to it. Treat failure as feedback, not a final verdict."

LESSON 3: LEGENDS LIFT OTHERS

"True legends," Vaathi said, "don't just shine; they light the way for others."

Examples of Collaboration Multiplying Success:

- Richard Branson: "Train people well enough so they can leave, but treat them well enough so they don't want to."
- Mahatma Gandhi: Empowered millions by making independence a collective effort.

"Legends don't hoard the spotlight, Kolaru," Vaathi added.

LESSON 4: INTEGRITY OUTLASTS EVERYTHING

"Short-term success built on shaky ethics," Vaathi warned, "collapses faster than a house of cards in a wind tunnel."

Example:

- Abraham Lincoln: Honesty fortified his leadership and legacy.
- Richard Nixon: Watergate overshadowed his achievements, proving ethical lapses dismantled trust.

"Integrity is simple," Vaathi explained. "When in doubt, ask: 'Would I be proud if this decision were public?' If not, rethink it."

A RADICAL IDEA: THE UNIVERSITY OF MISTAKES

"Imagine this," Vaathi mused, "a school where failure is the curriculum."

"Sounds depressing," Kolaru scoffed.

"No," Vaathi countered. "It's empowering. Think of it as a place where mistakes become blueprints for progress."

The Curriculum:

1. Case Studies: Analyse why ventures fail and extract lessons.

2. Post-Mortem Analysis: Turn failure into strategies for success.

3. Emotional Resilience: Rebuild confidence and grit after setbacks.

PRACTICAL WAYS TO LEARN FROM LEGENDS

"Want to learn from the greats?" Vaathi asked. "Start here."

1. Create a Legend Map: List five people you admire. For each, write one strategy to emulate and one mistake to avoid.

2. Document Your Failures: Treat setbacks as lessons, not verdicts.

3. Adapt, Don't Copy: Use brilliance as a blueprint, not a rulebook.

WRITE YOUR OWN LEGEND

"Legends aren't flawless," Vaathi said. "They're relentless. They own their mistakes, share their wisdom, and inspire others to do the same."

"And here's the best part," he added, leaning forward. "You don't need to be perfect to be a legend. You just need to keep moving forward."

As Rocky Balboa might say: "You're gonna get hit. That's a fact. But what do you do after the hit? That's what makes you a legend."

23

WISDOM AT WORK – MINDFUL LEADERSHIP AMID THE TIDES

MINDFULNESS: A BOARDROOM SURVIVAL GUIDE

"Vaathi," Kolaru began, sipping his tea with the air of someone about to declare something profound, "I've been hearing a lot about mindfulness. But how does sitting cross-legged and humming 'om' help when your boss is yelling, emails are piling up, and you're drowning in deadlines?"

Vaathi chuckled, leaning back in his chair. "Mindfulness isn't about humming, Kolaru. It's about clarity, focus, and showing up fully—even in the chaos, especially in the chaos."

"That sounds like motivational poster nonsense," Kolaru shot back. "Show me how this works in the real world."

"Alright," Vaathi said, his tone shifting to one of challenge. "Let's imagine your workplace is Yellowstone."

YELLOWSTONE AND WORKPLACE CHAOS

"Yellowstone?" Kolaru asked, raising an eyebrow.

"Yes, Yellowstone. It was in chaos once—imbalanced, overrun. Then, they reintroduced foxes into the ecosystem," Vaathi explained. "One small change restored the balance. Plants thrived, rivers stabilized, and everything came together."

"So, what you're saying is… I'm the fox?"

Vaathi smirked. "Or the chaos, depending on the day. But yes, mindful leadership is about finding the root cause and addressing it with clarity—not slapping a Band-Aid on the symptoms."

MINDFULNESS IN LEADERSHIP

"Fine, but mindfulness still sounds like something monks do on a mountain," Kolaru said.

"Not really," Vaathi replied. "Think of it as being fully present, like a surfer reading the waves. You don't control the ocean, but you adjust your stance to ride it better."

"And this helps… how?"

"For starters," Vaathi said, counting off on his fingers, "it keeps you from reacting impulsively, helps you focus on what truly matters, and builds trust. People follow clarity, not chaos."

Kolaru mulled it over. "Sounds like a lot of work. Can't I just wing it like usual?"

"You could," Vaathi said with a sly grin. "But then you'll stay stuck playing Whack-a-Mole with problems instead of actually leading."

THE EIGHTFOLD PATH AT WORK

"Let me give you a cheat sheet," Vaathi continued. "It's called the Eightfold Path, and it's all about applying clarity and purpose to everything you do."

1. **Right View – Seeing the Bigger Picture**

    "Ask yourself, 'What's the long-term goal here?' Without a clear view, you're just putting out fires."

    "Like when I fixed that printer jam but forgot the presentation deadline?" Kolaru asked.

    "Exactly."

2. **Right Intention – Acting with Integrity**

   "This is about aligning your actions with your values," Vaathi explained.

   "So, no more sneaky shortcuts?" Kolaru joked.

   "Unless you want to cut corners on trust, too," Vaathi shot back.

3. **Right Speech – Communicating Clearly and Kindly**

   "Criticism without clarity is cruelty," Vaathi said.

   "So, instead of saying, 'Your idea sucks,' I should say…?"

   "Try, 'Let's explore some challenges and find alternatives.'"

4. **Right Action – Leading by Example**

   "If you value punctuality, show up on time. Your team mirrors your actions," Vaathi explained.

   "So, no more complaining when I'm late?"

   "Precisely, Kolaru."

5. **Right Livelihood – Aligning Work with Values**

   "Work that aligns with values inspires loyalty," Vaathi added.

   "Like Tesla focusing on sustainability?"

   "Exactly. Vision drives trust."

6. **Right Effort – Balancing Ambition and Rest**

   "Success isn't about burnout, Kolaru. It's about impact."

   "So, working smarter, not harder?"

   "Now you're getting it."

7. **Right Mindfulness – Staying Present**

   "This is the heart of it. Focus fully on the moment."

   "Even during boring meetings?" Kolaru asked.

   "Especially then," Vaathi said, laughing.

8. Right Concentration – Prioritizing What Matters

"Deep focus leads to mastery," Vaathi concluded.

"So, no shiny distractions?"

"Ditch them, Kolaru."

MODERN LEADERSHIP DIMENSIONS

"Okay," Kolaru said, "but what about modern workplaces? They're not monasteries."

"True," Vaathi agreed. "That's where adaptability, emotional intelligence, and gratitude come in."

- Adaptability: "Think Netflix pivoting from DVDs to streaming."
- Emotional Intelligence: "Satya Nadella leading Microsoft with empathy."
- Conflict Resolution: "Turning tension into growth, like Toyota's A3 problem-solving."
- Gratitude: "Recognizing effort builds trust. Zappos does this brilliantly."

"Alright, give me the short version," Kolaru demanded.

"Fine," Vaathi said, smirking. "Here's what you need to remember:"

THE MONK'S SECRET (BUT NOT REALLY)

"So, I don't need to chant mantras or do yoga to be mindful?" Kolaru asked, a hint of relief in his voice.

"No," Vaathi said with a grin. "Just show up fully, think deeply, and lead with purpose. Clarity and compassion are your ultimate tools."

"Sounds… doable," Kolaru admitted. "But if I mess it up?"

"Then you reflect, learn, and try again," Vaathi replied. "Mindfulness isn't about being perfect, Kolaru. It's about being present."

"And maybe surf the occasional wave," Kolaru added, smirking.

"Now you're getting it."

24

SURFING THE EDGE OF RISK – BALANCING BOLDNESS WITH CAUTION

RISK: THE LEADER'S UNAVOIDABLE WAVE

"Kolaru," Vaathi began, swirling his coffee like he was about to deliver a prophecy, "risk isn't something you can escape."

Kolaru sighed, slumping in his chair. "I was hoping you'd say something like, 'Risk is overrated,' or 'Just stay in the shallow end.'

Vaathi chuckled. "If you want to lead, you'll have to ride the waves, not dodge them. But don't mistake risk for recklessness. Great leaders don't dive headfirst. They paddle with precision, reading the tides before taking the leap."

"So, how do I know which waves to ride?" Kolaru asked, skeptically.

"That's the art of calculated risk-taking," Vaathi said. "It's not about avoiding risk but about riding with boldness, preparation, and control."

UNDERSTANDING RISK: APPETITE, MITIGATION, AND THE MYTH OF RISK-AVERSION

1. Risk Appetite: Knowing Your Limits

   "Every leader has a different tolerance for uncertainty, Kolaru. The key is knowing how far you can go without capsizing."

   "Sounds simple enough," Kolaru replied. "But what if I don't know my limits?"

   "Ask yourself these questions," Vaathi said:

   - How much can I afford to lose without jeopardizing my core goals?
   - Does this risk align with my values?
   - What's my backup plan if it goes south?

2. The Three Levels of Risk Appetite

   - **Conservative:** Prioritizes stability over bold moves.

     Example: Companies in mature industries focusing on steady growth.

   - **Moderate:** Balances caution with ambition.

     Example: Testing new products while safeguarding existing revenue streams.

   - **Aggressive:** All in for transformative rewards.

     Example: Startups betting everything on disruptive ideas.

   "Risk appetite isn't static," Vaathi added. "A bold move in one area might be reckless in another."

3. Risk Mitigation: Protecting Yourself While Taking the Leap

   "Here's the secret: mitigation isn't about avoiding risk but about reducing the damage if things go wrong."

   Vaathi outlined four strategies:

   1. Avoidance: Walk away if the downside is catastrophic.

      Example: Skipping investments in unfamiliar industries.

2. Reduction: Minimize the potential impact.

   Example: Launching a pilot project before a full-scale rollout.

3. Transfer: Share the risk.

   Example: Partnering with experts or outsourcing.

4. Acceptance: Prepare for manageable risks.

   Example: Launching a bold campaign despite uncertainty.

THE MYTH OF RISK-AVERSION

"Let me burst your bubble, Kolaru," Vaathi said. "Avoiding risk entirely? That's a myth."

"Sounds convenient," Kolaru quipped.

"Not really. Life itself is a risk. Avoiding it comes with its own price."

Three Reasons Risk Aversion is a Myth:

1. Opportunity Cost: Playing it safe often costs more than taking the leap.
   Example: Kodak clung to film and missed the digital revolution.

2. Uncertainty is Constant: No matter how safe you play, variables remain.
   Example: Even the safest investments face inflation risks.

3. Paralysis Costs More Than Action: Overthinking stalls progress.
   Example: Hesitating to adopt new tech can leave you irrelevant.

THE ART OF ASSESSING THE WAVE

"Not every wave is worth riding, Kolaru. The trick is knowing which ones matter," Vaathi explained.

Before You Leap, Ask yourself:

1. What's the worst that could happen?

2. What's the potential reward?

3. Am I prepared for this ride?

Creating a Risk-Reward Matrix

"Here's your cheat sheet," Vaathi said, sketching a simple grid.

Risk/Reward	Low Reward	High Reward
Low Risk	Skip it.	Sweet Spot – Go for it.
High Risk	Avoid it.	Proceed cautiously.

"Stick to the sweet spots and tread cautiously with high-stakes opportunities," Vaathi advised.

LESSONS FROM THE LEGENDS

"Think of it this way, Kolaru," Vaathi said, leaning in. "Legends don't ride every wave—they ride the right waves."

Example:

- Steve Jobs: The iPhone was a bold bet, but meticulous planning made it revolutionary.

- Elon Musk: Faced near-bankruptcy multiple times, yet his optimism and grit kept him afloat.

- Rosa Parks: Her refusal to give up her seat was a calculated risk that ignited a movement.

PREPARING FOR THE WIPEOUT

"Even the best surfers fall," Vaathi said. "The difference? They know how to recover."

1. Backup Plans Are Lifelines: Always have contingencies.

2. Own Your Failures: Admitting mistakes builds credibility.

3. Celebrate the Wipeout: Each failure sharpens instincts for the next wave.

"Remember Blockbuster?" Vaathi asked. "Their wipeout came because they refused to adapt. Ignoring risks can be worse than taking them."

BOLDNESS WITH HUMILITY: KNOWING WHEN TO RETREAT

"Courage isn't just about leaping; it's about knowing when to hold back," Vaathi said.

How to Retreat Wisely:

1. Study the Ocean: Observe trends and patterns before acting.

2. Trust Your Gut: Experience sharpens intuition—use it.

3. Communicate Clearly: Whether advancing or retreating, transparency builds trust.

"Jeff Bezos waited years before launching Amazon Prime," Vaathi said. "That patience made it a game-changer."

THE MANIFESTO OF RISK-TAKING

"Calculated risk-taking isn't gambling, Kolaru—it's a craft," Vaathi concluded. "You ride boldly into the waves you're ready for, learn from your wipeouts, and steer toward your vision."

"And if I miscalculate?" Kolaru asked.

"Then you get up, adjust, and paddle out again," Vaathi replied. "Because leadership isn't about avoiding danger—it's about riding the waves that matter with clarity, courage, and control."

IGNITING INFINITE POSSIBILITIES

(Unleash the Creator within and Break Through Every Wall)

Creativity isn't an exclusive club for artists, inventors, or the "gifted". It's the lifeline of progress, the force that transforms the ordinary into the extraordinary. Picture it as the ocean—wild, unpredictable, and bursting with waves of innovation. And those walls you think can't be breached? Creativity is the wave that smashes right through them.

Kolaru squinted, arms crossed. "Alright, Vaathi, I hear the poetry. But not everyone's built to surf this so-called wave."

Vaathi leaned back, smirking. "That's where you're wrong, Kolaru. Creativity isn't some rare gift—it's a mindset. It's daring to ask, 'What if?' and refusing to stop at the first obstacle."

THE KEY WAS NEVER LOST

"Think about that locked door you pass every day," Vaathi continued. "You've jiggled the handle, assumed it's locked, and moved on. But what if the key has been in your pocket all along?"

"Yeah, but what if it isn't?" Kolaru shot back.

"Then you haven't checked hard enough," Vaathi said. "Creativity isn't about finding something new—it's about rediscovering what you already have. Somewhere along the way, we all buried it under rules, self-doubt, and fear of failure."

"So, it's like dusting off some old, forgotten part of yourself?"

"Exactly," Vaathi nodded. "You don't need anything extra. The tools are already there. You just have to use them."

THE POWER OF REBELLION AND 'WHAT IF?'

"All great creativity begins with rebellion," Vaathi explained, tapping his cup. "Not the kind where you just break things for fun, but the kind that questions what's broken and imagines something better."

"Sounds dangerous," Kolaru said.

"It can be," Vaathi admitted. "But rebellion without purpose? That's just noise. True creativity is a balance between chaos and control, courage and caution. It's about looking at the rules and daring to say, 'What if?'"

PLAY: THE FORGOTTEN REVOLUTION

"Okay," Kolaru said, raising an eyebrow. "What's with all this talk about 'play'? Isn't that just a waste of time?"

"Play isn't frivolous, Kolaru—it's revolutionary," Vaathi countered. "It's how you ask the questions no one else will and see connections no one else can. When's the last time you let yourself play?"

"Play? I barely have time to breathe, let alone goof off."

"And that," Vaathi said, pointing, "is the problem. We were told to 'get serious,' and somewhere along the way, we forgot that play fuels creativity. If you want to think outside the box, you've got to stop living inside it."

WHAT THIS PART IS ABOUT

"This part isn't about handing you new tools," Vaathi explained. "It's about showing you the ones you already have. It's about unlocking doors you thought were dead ends. It's about breaking the rules—not for chaos, but for creation."

"Rules are meant to be broken?" Kolaru teased.

"When they're holding you back, yes," Vaathi said. "But creativity doesn't thrive on recklessness. It thrives on curiosity, courage, and the willingness to fail boldly."

THE LEAP INTO INFINITE POSSIBILITIES

"The stage is set," Vaathi said, "but the curtain is yours to pull back. You don't need to become someone else to create—you just need to rediscover the magic already in you. The walls you see? They're illusions. And the key? It's right there, waiting for you to use it."

"Alright, Vaathi," Kolaru said, smirking. "Let's say I find this key. What do I do with it?"

"You open the door, Kolaru," Vaathi replied. "You dream boldly, fail boldly, and redefine what's possible."

It's time to ride the waves of imagination, break through every wall, and create the extraordinary.

"Ready to paddle out?" Vaathi asked.

"Ready," Kolaru said with a grin.

25 CREATIVITY UNLEASHED: RIDING IMAGINATION'S SWELLS

Creativity isn't reserved for a special few—it's in everyone, waiting to be unlocked. It's not about sudden epiphanies or eccentric brilliance; it's the ability to see what others overlook, to ask "Why not?" when everyone else says, "That's impossible."

"Creativity is about connecting the dots," Vaathi said. "The trick is seeing the dots no one else notices."

"Sounds philosophical," Kolaru muttered. "What are these 'dots' anyway?"

"They're everywhere," Vaathi replied. "Frustrations, mistakes, missed opportunities. Like Post-It Notes. Arthur Fry wasn't trying to change the world—he just wanted his bookmarks to stop slipping. The spark? A failed glue experiment. What others saw as useless, he turned into a genius."

"So, it's not about brilliance?" Kolaru asked, skeptical.

"It's about curiosity," Vaathi said. "And the courage to try something ridiculous."

CONSTRAINTS: THE UNSUNG HERO OF CREATIVITY

"Ever notice how you come up with the best solutions when your options are limited?" Vaathi asked.

"Like when I had to patch that leaking pipe with duct tape and sheer panic?" Kolaru smirked.

"Exactly," Vaathi laughed. "Constraints force innovation. Look at Apollo 13. NASA engineers used duct tape, socks, and cardboard to save the astronauts. When you can't have everything, you learn to work with what you've got."

"So, constraints are good?"

"Necessary," Vaathi corrected. "Too many resources make you complacent. Too few push you to greatness."

THE MYTH OF BIG IDEAS

"Everyone's chasing big ideas," Vaathi said. "But small ones often have the biggest impact."

"Like what?" Kolaru leaned forward, intrigued.

"Think about cup holders in cars. Not exactly life-changing, right? But they solve everyday frustration. Compare that to Ada Lovelace's vision of the first computer program. Both changed lives—just in different ways."

"So, do small ideas count?"

"Big or small doesn't matter," Vaathi replied. "Impact does. Stop waiting for your 'aha' moment and start noticing the little things."

THE ENEMIES OF CREATIVITY

"You know what kills creativity?" Vaathi asked, leaning closer.

"Lack of talent?" Kolaru guessed.

"Nope. Fear, procrastination, and perfectionism."

"Fear I get," Kolaru said. "But procrastination? Isn't that just waiting for inspiration?"

"That's the excuse," Vaathi said. "Inspiration comes after action, not before. You have to start—even if it's messy."

"And perfectionism?"

"The biggest trap," Vaathi said. "It sounds noble but keeps you stuck. 'Perfect' is the enemy of 'done.' Aim for progress, not perfection."

CREATIVITY UNDER PRESSURE

"Ever notice how you get resourceful during a crisis?" Vaathi asked.

"Like when I crammed a week's work into one night?" Kolaru grinned.

"Exactly. Pressure sparks brilliance. During WWII, scientists recycled penicillin from patients' urine because supply was scarce. Gross? Sure. But it saved lives. Chaos forces clarity."

"So, should I embrace chaos?"

"Not chaos," Vaathi corrected. "Opportunity within chaos."

PLAY: THE FORGOTTEN SUPERPOWER

"When was the last time you let yourself play, Kolaru?"

"Play? I'm not five," Kolaru scoffed.

"That's the problem," Vaathi said. "Play isn't childish—it's revolutionary. Lin-Manuel Miranda came up with Hamilton because he let curiosity guide him. Play lets you explore without judgment."

"Fine," Kolaru said. "I'll go play in the sand."

"Not literally, but sure," Vaathi chuckled.

ABSURDITY SPARKS BRILLIANCE

"Ever had a ridiculous idea?" Vaathi asked.

"Plenty," Kolaru admitted. "Most of them get laughed off."

"That's the point," Vaathi said. "Absurd ideas often lead to breakthroughs. James Dyson built over 5,000 prototypes for his vacuum. Absurd persistence? Yes. Revolutionary results? Absolutely."

"So, I should lean into my crazy ideas?"

"With purpose," Vaathi said. "Somewhere between absurd and genius lies brilliance."

THE MAGIC OF REST

"Do you know where your best ideas come from?" Vaathi asked.

"Hard work?"

"Nope. Rest," Vaathi replied. "Lin-Manuel Miranda dreamed up Hamilton on the subway, not at his desk. Your brain connects dots when it's not focused on working."

"So, daydreaming isn't laziness?"

"Not at all," Vaathi said. "It's incubation. Give your brain space, and it'll surprise you."

RIDING IMAGINATION'S SWELLS

"Creativity isn't about waiting for inspiration," Vaathi said. "It's about showing up, trying, failing, and trying again."

"Even if I fall flat on my face?" Kolaru asked.

"Especially then," Vaathi said with a grin. "The next Post-It Note or Hamilton isn't made by someone smarter—it's made by someone who begins."

"And if I start paddling the wrong wave?"

"Then you adjust," Vaathi replied. "Creativity isn't perfect—it's messy, exhilarating, and yours to claim."

The ocean's waiting. Will you paddle out?

26 MINDSETS AND HABITS: PERFECTING YOUR CREATIVE SURF STANCE

Creativity isn't some divine spark reserved for the lucky few—it's a skill you build, like mastering the perfect surf stance. You fall, you adjust, and you ride again. Think of it as cooking: burn a few dishes, and soon you're serving meals that wow. Creativity thrives on consistent habits and a mindset that treats failure not as an end but as a guide.

"Alright, Vaathi," Kolaru said, arms crossed. "But what if I'm not the 'creative' type?"

"Everyone's creative, Kolaru," Vaathi replied. "Creativity isn't magic. It's curiosity in action. It's about showing up, experimenting, and learning from every wipeout."

MINDSETS THAT SPARK CREATIVITY

1. **Adopt a Growth Mindset:** "Remember when you learned to walk, Kolaru?" Vaathi asked. "You didn't care how many times you fell. You just kept going."

   "Yeah, but now failing feels… bigger," Kolaru admitted.

   "That's the problem. Adults fear looking foolish, but failure is feedback—it's how you grow. Look at Kalam's early rocket failures. They didn't stop him—they set the stage for India's space program."

2. **Let Emotions Be Your Rocket Fuel:** "Creativity runs on emotions—raw and unfiltered," Vaathi said. "Heartbreak, joy, anger—use it all."

"So, I turn my bad mood into a masterpiece?" Kolaru asked, smirking.

"Exactly. Gulzar did. His poetry captures emotion so vividly it feels like he's speaking to your soul."

3. **Find Your Flow:** "Flow is that magical zone where distractions disappear, and time melts," Vaathi explained.

"Sounds rare," Kolaru said.

"Not if you practice. M.S. Subbulakshmi didn't just wake up legendary— she worked until flow became second nature."

4. **Let Curiosity Be Your Compass:** "As a kid, you probably asked 'why' a hundred times a day. When did you stop?" Vaathi asked.

"When people got annoyed," Kolaru muttered.

"Bad trade," Vaathi replied. "Curiosity drives creativity. The Jaipur Foot prosthetic? It exists because someone asked, 'Why can't this be affordable and functional?'"

HABITS THAT BUILD CREATIVE MOMENTUM

1. **Block Time for Creativity:** "You wouldn't cancel a doctor's appointment," Vaathi said. "Why cancel time for creativity?"

"Easier said than done," Kolaru replied.

"Ruskin Bond writes every morning. That's how he has written for decades. Make it sacred, and the work will follow."

2. **Capture Every Idea:** "The best ideas strike at random—don't trust your brain to remember them," Vaathi said.

"So, should I start doodling on napkins like R.K. Laxman?"

"Or just use your phone. The method doesn't matter. Capturing does."

3. **Embrace Constraints:** "Constraints aren't blocks, they're boosts," Vaathi said.

"How does having less help?" Kolaru asked.

"Look at Satyajit Ray. He made Pather Panchali on a shoestring budget. Creativity thrives when you have to innovate to make things work."

4. **Deadlines Are Your Frenemies:** "I hate deadlines," Kolaru groaned.

"They force you to finish, even when perfectionism whispers 'wait,'" Vaathi said. "Messy drafts beat unfinished dreams every time."

5. **Shape Your Environment:** "Your workspace is your launchpad," Vaathi said. "Make it inspiring, not stifling."

"Like Tagore's Shantiniketan?" Kolaru asked.

"Exactly. Your surroundings shape your output—choose them wisely."

RIDE THE CREATIVE WAVE

"Creativity isn't about waiting for lightning to strike," Vaathi said. "It's about showing up, falling, and getting better with every attempt."

"And if I wipe out?" Kolaru asked.

"You adjust and paddle out again," Vaathi replied with a grin. "Creativity isn't about the perfect wave—it's about riding the ones that come your way."

"Alright, Vaathi. I'll give it a shot."

"Good," Vaathi said. "Because the ocean's waiting, and your board's ready. Start paddling."

COLLABORATION WAVES – SMOOTH RIDES, NO CRASHES

27

Collaboration is like tandem surfing: when everyone's in sync, you ride the wave beautifully. But when someone paddles the wrong way or refuses to move, you all wipe out, and the perfect wave disappears into the horizon.

"Collaboration feels like a buzzword," Kolaru muttered. "Most of the time, it's just chaos with more people involved."

Vaathi smirked. "That's because teamwork without structure is chaos. Collaboration isn't about cramming people into a room and hoping for magic— it's about trust, alignment, and communication. When it works, though, it's transformative."

Take Amul's famous "Utterly Butterly" campaigns. The wit, cultural relevance, and staying power weren't the work of one genius. It was the result of a team that understood the power of a shared vision and collective creativity.

COLLABORATION: YOUR CREATIVITY MULTIPLIER

Collaboration doesn't just add creativity but multiplies it. A team's combined perspectives create solutions no individual could dream of alone.

"Think of collaboration like adding Mentos to Coke," Vaathi said. "It's explosive—if handled right."

Kolaru raised an eyebrow. "And if handled wrong?"

"Sticky disaster," Vaathi replied.

Real Story: ISRO's Mars Orbiter Mission wasn't just about brilliant minds. It was about a team paddling in the same direction with perfect alignment, even on a shoestring budget. That's the power of true collaboration.

THE CORE OF COLLABORATION

1. Trust: The Foundation: Without trust, collaboration is just people tolerating each other. Trust means your team feels safe to challenge ideas, admit mistakes, and root for each other.

    "Remember M.S. Dhoni?" Vaathi asked. "He didn't just lead the Indian cricket team—he trusted them to take risks. That trust empowered players to give their best, even under pressure."

    Pro Tip: Start meetings with "highlight reels". Sharing small wins builds rapport and sets a positive tone.

2. Alignment: Paddling Together: "If everyone's paddling in different directions, you'll wipe out," Vaathi said. "Alignment is about shared goals and clear roles."

    "Easier said than done," Kolaru grumbled. "What happens when people say they're aligned but aren't?"

    "Then it's your job to bring clarity," Vaathi replied. "Misalignment often comes from fuzzy goals."

    Real Story: ISRO's historic mission succeeded because every team member, from scientists to engineers, understood their part in the larger goal.

    Pro Tip: Before starting any project, ask: What's the main goal? Who's doing what? How will success be measured?

3. Communication: The Lifeline: Miscommunication is the iceberg that sinks great ideas. Clear, empathetic communication keeps the team aligned and prevents avoidable conflicts.

"Think about Mumbai's Dabbawallas," Vaathi said. "They deliver 200,000 lunchboxes daily with near-perfect accuracy because their communication system is simple and consistent."

Kolaru leaned back. "I guess 'simple' beats the 1,000 emails people send these days."

"Exactly," Vaathi nodded. "Overcommunication isn't clarity—it's clutter."

AVOIDING COLLABORATION WIPEOUTS

1. Groupthink: "When everyone agrees too quickly, you lose innovation," Vaathi warned. "Assign a 'devil's advocate' to challenge the status quo."

   Real Story: Dr. Verghese Kurien, the man behind India's White Revolution, disrupted conventional thinking by asking questions no one else dared to.

2. Uneven Workloads: "Nothing kills morale faster than some people doing all the work," Vaathi said. "Define roles clearly—who's responsible, accountable, consulted, and informed."

   "RACI charts again?" Kolaru groaned.

   "They work for a reason," Vaathi replied. "And don't forget to celebrate contributions—it keeps the team motivated."

3. Conflict: "Conflict's unavoidable," Vaathi said, shrugging. "But it doesn't have to be destructive. Frame it as an opportunity to refine ideas."

   "Or just argue until someone gives up," Kolaru joked.

   "That's not conflict—that's drama," Vaathi retorted. "Focus on solving problems, not attacking people."

HOW TO STRENGTHEN COLLABORATION

- Brainstorm Roulette: Pair team members from different departments for fresh perspectives.

- Work-in-Progress Reviews: Share drafts early for constructive feedback.

- Surf Checks: After a project, hold a session to reflect on what worked, what didn't, and what's next.

RIDE THE WAVE TOGETHER

Collaboration is messy, unpredictable, and sometimes frustrating. But when it clicks, it's magic. The best waves aren't ridden solo—they're shared rides filled with occasional crashes and the joy of creating something extraordinary together. "So," Kolaru said, smirking, "teamwork isn't about herding cats but about teaching them to surf?"

"Exactly," Vaathi replied. "Trust your team, align your goals, and paddle out together. The waves won't wait forever." The water's ready; you're not paddling alone this time.

BUSINESS CREATIVITY: IDEAS THAT POWER THE SURF ENGINE

28

CREATIVITY: THE ULTIMATE BUSINESS ENGINE

In the world of work, creativity is like the surf engine: without it, you're left paddling while competitors glide effortlessly past, riding waves of innovation. But here's the hard truth—creativity isn't tossing jargon-laden "big ideas" into a brainstorming abyss or slapping neon charts onto PowerPoint slides.

True creativity solves real problems, challenges norms, and drives bold execution. It thrives in chaos, disrupts comfort zones, and leaves no room for half-hearted efforts.

In short, creativity is messy. That's why most people (and companies) avoid it like a storm on the horizon. But here's the catch—avoiding the storm doesn't make it disappear. The only thing scarier than disruption is irrelevance.

THE CLASH: VAATHI VS. KOLARU

Picture this: a high-stakes boardroom meeting. The topic? A new product launch that could make or break the company's future.

Kolaru strolls in late, carrying his laptop like it's Excalibur, and starts with a smirk. "Ladies and gentlemen, allow me to introduce a revolutionary concept," he begins, loading up a dazzling PowerPoint deck.

The slides are peppered with words he's recently picked up from The Hindu newspaper and his latest Netflix binge: "synergistic ecosystems," "disruptive innovation," and "future-ready paradigms." For five whole minutes, Kolaru dazzles the room with his jargon-filled monologue, his voice oozing confidence.

But then Vaathi speaks up, calm and collected. "Kolaru," he says, folding his arms. "This revolutionary concept of yours—is it an actual idea or just a collection of fancy words?"

Kolaru grins. "Oh, it's much more than that, Vaathi. It's a game-changer."

"Really?" Vaathi raises an eyebrow. "What's the problem you're solving? What's the execution plan? How does this idea impact our customers?"

Kolaru fumbles. "Well, you see… the big picture is—"

Vaathi interrupts with a tone sharp enough to cut steel. "No big picture. Details. Right now."

The room falls silent. Kolaru glances at the screen, then back at Vaathi. "It's a work in progress," he mumbles.

"Exactly," Vaathi says, leaning forward. "You've brought us chaos disguised as creativity. Let me show you how creativity works when it's disciplined."

WHY CREATIVITY IS YOUR ULTIMATE ADVANTAGE

Vaathi stands up and gestures toward the board. "In today's world, creativity isn't just a buzzword—it's survival," he explains. "Take Netflix, for example. They didn't just pivot from DVDs to streaming—they reimagined entertainment itself. They asked the right questions, took bold risks, and executed flawlessly. That's creativity with purpose."

Kolaru leans back in his chair, arms crossed. "Netflix was lucky," he mutters.

"Luck?" Vaathi's voice carries the weight of thunder. "Luck didn't build their infrastructure, secure global streaming rights, or create original content that changed the industry. Luck had nothing to do with it—discipline did."

THE ANATOMY OF BUSINESS CREATIVITY

"Let's break it down," Vaathi continues. "Creativity is a process, not a magic trick. Here's how it works when done right."

1. **Clarity Before Creativity**

   "Creativity without a clear problem to solve is just noise," Vaathi explains. "Define the challenge first."

   Kolaru interjects. "But what about thinking outside the box?"

   Vaathi smirks. "Thinking outside the box doesn't mean ignoring the box entirely. It means understanding what's inside it first."

2. **Balance Big Ideas with Execution**

   "Dreaming big is easy," Vaathi says, turning to Kolaru. "Delivering is the hard part. Tesla didn't just imagine electric cars—they built factories and optimized supply chains. That's execution."

   Kolaru leans forward. "But big ideas are what inspire people."

   "And execution is what keeps them inspired," Vaathi retorts. "No one's inspired by a dream that never becomes reality."

3. **Overcoming Creativity Barriers**

   Vaathi points at Kolaru. "Your barrier, Kolaru, is that you think excuses are solutions."

   Kolaru opens his mouth to argue, but Vaathi cuts him off. "Stop imagining roadblocks. Start clearing them."

BUILDING A CREATIVE CULTURE

"Creativity isn't just an individual effort," Vaathi explains. "It's a team sport. And the environment you create determines whether your team thrives or stumbles."

1. **Psychological Safety**

   "Creativity dies in fear," Vaathi says. "Teams need to feel safe to share bold ideas."

Kolaru snickers. "So, do we just let everyone say whatever they want?"

"No," Vaathi replies, his voice firm. "But we let them speak without fear of judgment. Pixar's Braintrust thrives because everyone—regardless of rank—can critique ideas openly."

2. Diversity Fuels Creativity

"The best ideas come from diverse perspectives," Vaathi continues. "Zomato's campaigns resonate because they understand their audience, from urban millennials to small-town foodies. Diversity is their superpower."

STORYTELLING: THE SECRET SAUCE FOR SELLING IDEAS

As the discussion winds down, Vaathi turns to Kolaru. Here's something we agree on: people remember stories, not data. But the difference is that you use stories to distract, while I use them to inspire action."

They gesture to the screen. "When Steve Jobs unveiled the iPhone, he didn't just list features—he told a story about the future. That's how you sell ideas."

THE SURF ENGINE FRAMEWORK FOR BUSINESS CREATIVITY

"To ride the waves of business creativity, think of this as your surf engine," Vaathi concludes:

1. Ideation: Generate bold, unconventional ideas.

2. Iteration: Test, refine and adapt.

3. Integration: Combine diverse perspectives into cohesive solutions.

4. Execution: Deliver with precision and urgency.

RIDING THE BUSINESS SURF ENGINE

As the meeting wraps up, Kolaru slouches in his chair, his ego visibly bruised. Vaathi, on the other hand, stands tall. "Business creativity isn't about chasing every wave—it's about catching the right ones with precision, courage, and focus," he says.

By fostering bold ideas, dismantling barriers, and building a culture of innovation, you don't just ride the wave of creativity—you set the tide for others to follow.

Vaathi looks around the room. "So, the real question isn't, 'Can your business afford to be creative?' It's, 'Can it afford not to be?'"

29

CURIOSITY MEETS PLAY: RIDING WAVES TO NEW SHORES

THE POWER OF CURIOSITY AND PLAY

Curiosity and play are two things adults seem to abandon faster than their childhood diaries. Yet, these so-called "frivolities" are the secret weapons behind breakthroughs. While curiosity whispers, "What's out there?" play shouts back, "Let's mess around and see!" Together, they're the engine of creativity and the gateway to innovation.

Here's the kicker: you're not going to unlock bold ideas by staring at a spreadsheet or forcing yourself into a "serious brainstorming session." Magic happens when curiosity roams freely, and you give yourself permission to experiment—without judgment or fear of failure.

Vaathi and Kolaru Debate Curiosity

Kolaru leans back in his chair, spinning a pen between his fingers. "Curiosity is overrated," he declares. "It's just an excuse to waste time digging into rabbit holes."

Vaathi, perched calmly across the table, raises an eyebrow. "And where do you think breakthroughs come from? Staring at spreadsheets?"

Kolaru smirks. "Breakthroughs come from analysis, not daydreaming."

"Analysis follows curiosity," Vaathi replies sharply. "Without curiosity, you wouldn't even know what to analyze."

The tension in the room thickens, but Vaathi leans forward, a slight smile forming. "Let me show you what happens when curiosity meets play."

THE CURIOSITY COMPASS: ASKING BETTER QUESTIONS

"Great ideas don't come from having all the answers," Vaathi explains. "They come from asking the right questions. Curious minds don't stop at 'Why is this broken?'—they push further with 'What happens if we rebuild it from scratch?'"

Real Story: IDEO and the Shopping Cart Revolution

"When IDEO redesigned the shopping cart, they didn't start with aesthetics or cost-cutting," Vaathi continues. "They asked, 'What do shoppers hate most?' That simple question sparked innovations like detachable baskets and safer designs."

Kolaru crosses his arms. "That's just design thinking. Nothing groundbreaking."

Vaathi shoots him a look. "Tell me, Kolaru, when was the last time you asked a 'What if' question?"

Kolaru hesitates. "Last week, I asked, 'What if we didn't waste time on these creative exercises?'"

Vaathi sighs. "Exactly my point."

PLAY: THE UNSUNG HERO OF INNOVATION

"If curiosity is the compass," Vaathi continues, "then play is the paddle that keeps the boat moving. Playfulness lowers the stakes, unlocks new ideas, and reminds us why creativity is fun—even when failure shows up to the party."

Real Story: LEGO's Revival Through Play

"In the early 2000s, LEGO was drowning in debt. Their solution? Lean into their essence: play. They launched LEGO movies and sets for adults, proving that play isn't just for kids—it's a strategy for growth."

Kolaru chuckles. "Play? For adults? Isn't that just… procrastination?"

Vaathi shakes his head. "No, Kolaru. Procrastination is avoiding the problem. Play is attacking it from unexpected angles."

WHEN CURIOSITY MEETS PLAY: MAGIC HAPPENS

"Let's make this real," Vaathi says, pointing at the whiteboard.

1. The "What If" Game

    "This simple game removes limits and sparks possibilities," Vaathi explains.

    Example:

    o   "What if our app predicted trends instead of just tracking them?"

    o   "What if our team retreats doubled as community events?"

    Real Story: Airbnb's Origin

    "Airbnb started with a playful question: 'What if people rented out their spare rooms to strangers?' That one question turned into a $113 billion platform."

    Kolaru shrugs. "Sounds like dumb luck."

    "Luck?" Vaathi smirks. "More like curiosity and execution."

2. **Playful Prototyping**

    "Great ideas don't start polished," Vaathi continues. "They start messy. Prototypes let you fail fast and learn faster."

    Real Story: James Dyson's Vacuum Saga

    "Dyson created over 5,000 failed prototypes before perfecting his iconic vacuum. Each failure was a step closer to success."

    Kolaru raises an eyebrow. "5,000 failures? Sounds inefficient."

    Vaathi smiles. "And yet, he built a billion-dollar company. How's your perfect record doing, Kolaru?"

3. **Gamify the Process**

    "Why slog through work when you can turn it into a game?" Vaathi asks. "Gamification sparks creativity by making the process fun."

    Example: "Turn brainstorming into a competition: 'Who can pitch the wildest idea in 10 minutes?'"

    Kolaru leans forward, intrigued. "So, you're saying I can make my team work harder… by playing games?"

    Vaathi nods. "Exactly. But only if you can resist ruining it with overthinking."

BUILDING A CULTURE OF CURIOSITY AND PLAY

"Curiosity and play aren't individual efforts," Vaathi says. "They thrive in a supportive environment."

1. **Create Safe Spaces**

    "Judgment kills curiosity faster than a typo in a job application," Vaathi explains. "Google X's Moonshot Factory celebrates failed projects as milestones. That's how you nurture bold exploration."

    Pro Tip: Start meetings by sharing your most ridiculous idea to show bold thinking is welcome.

2. **Cross-Department Curiosity**

    "Collaboration across disciplines sparks fresh perspectives," Vaathi continues. "Pixar's magic happens because animators and engineers work hand in hand, blending storytelling with tech."

3. **Celebrate the Process, Not Just the Outcome**

    "Stop rewarding only polished results. Celebrate the messy, awkward, experimental middle."

    Pro Tip: Start a "Curiosity Fund" for passion projects—no pressure for immediate results.

REDISCOVER WONDER AND AWE

Vaathi leans back, looking out of the window. "When was the last time you marveled at something simple? A sunset, the rhythm of waves, or even a child's laughter?"

Kolaru scoffs. "We're here to talk about work, not poetry."

Vaathi smiles. "Exactly. And that's why you're stuck."

THE PLAYFUL EDGE

Curiosity and play aren't optional extras; they're the spark plugs of innovation. They challenge norms, inject joy into the creative process, and open doors where others see only walls.

Vaathi turns to Kolaru one last time. "The next big wave isn't waiting for your seriousness. It's waiting for your imagination to take the leap."

Kolaru sighs, then smirks. "Fine. Let's play."

30

CREATIVE PROBLEM-SOLVING: THE SURFER'S AGILE MINDSET

SURFING BEYOND THE WAVE: THE ART OF CREATIVE PROBLEM-SOLVING

Life doesn't hand you neatly packaged problems. Instead, it delivers tangled puzzles wrapped in chaos, garnished with a ticking clock. But here's the kicker—problems are just opportunities to wear bad disguises. The secret to unmasking them? Creative problem-solving.

Think of it like surfing. You can't control the waves but can master how to ride them. It's not about brute force; it's about balance, agility, and spotting hidden opportunities. Every wipeout is feedback, every wave is a lesson, and every solution is your chance to ride smarter and bolder.

THE VAATHI AND KOLARU SHOWDOWN: PROBLEM-SOLVING EDITION

In a corner office filled with tension, Kolaru slouches in his chair, swirling a pen between his fingers. "Problems are just an excuse for overthinking," he declares.

Vaathi, seated calmly across the table, raises an eyebrow. "And your solution is to ignore them until they disappear?"

Kolaru smirks. "No, I solve them efficiently—do something, anything, and move on."

Vaathi leans forward, his gaze piercing. "Ah, yes. The Kolaru method: patch the leak without checking if the pipe is broken. You might save time now, but you'll drown later."

The room goes quiet. Kolaru clears his throat. "Fine. Teach me your magical method."

STEP 1: DEFINE THE PROBLEM—GUESSING GETS YOU NOWHERE

"Here's the first rule of problem-solving," Vaathi begins. "Define your problem with painful precision. Misdiagnosing is like paddling hard in a kiddie pool— lots of effort, zero progress."

Real Story: Toyota's "Five Whys"

"When Toyota faced production issues, they didn't stop at surface-level fixes," Vaathi explains. "They asked 'Why?' five times to uncover the root cause. A broken machine wasn't the problem—a flawed supplier process was."

Kolaru shrugs. "Sounds tedious."

Vaathi smirks. "And yet, it works."

Pro Tip: Write your problem in one jargon-free sentence. If it doesn't make you say, 'Oh, duh,' dig deeper.

STEP 2: THINK SIDEWAYS—WHEN THE OBVIOUS PATH FAILS

"When the front door's locked, try the window," Vaathi says. "Lateral thinking is about uncovering unconventional solutions."

Example: Reimagine umbrellas. Most focus on better materials. But someone asked, 'How can we make rain fun?' Cue raincoats with built-in speakers.

Real Story: Airbnb's $100 Billion Idea

"'Strangers sleeping in your home' sounded ridiculous—until Airbnb redefined global travel," Vaathi explains.

Kolaru raises an eyebrow. "That was luck."

"Luck or curiosity?" Vaathi counters.

STEP 3: PROTOTYPE FAST—TALK LESS, DO MORE

"Stop overthinking and start building," Vaathi advises. "Even if your prototype is held together with duct tape, it's better than endless discussions."

Real Story: Dyson's Vacuum Marathon

"James Dyson didn't nail his vacuum on the first try," Vaathi says. "It took over 5,000 prototypes. Progress is born in messy iterations."

Pro Tip: Forget perfection. Build fast, fail fast, and learn faster.

STEP 4: EMBRACE CONSTRAINTS—BECAUSE LIMITS SPARK INGENUITY

"Constraints aren't obstacles; they're creativity's secret ingredient," Vaathi declares.

Real Story: Apollo 13's DIY Solution

"When NASA's oxygen system failed, engineers saved the crew using duct tape, socks, and sheer brilliance."

Kolaru grins. "Finally, duct tape gets the respect it deserves."

STEP 5: FLIP THE SCRIPT—INVERT EVERYTHING

"Sometimes, the best solutions come from flipping the problem upside down," Vaathi explains.

Example: Instead of asking, "How do we get customers to stay?" ask, "What would make them leave?" Then do the opposite.

Real Story: Netflix's Streaming Revolution

"Netflix didn't ask, 'How do we rent DVDs faster?' They flipped the script: 'What if people didn't need DVDs at all?'"

STEP 6: ADD EMPATHY—SOLUTIONS NEED TO FEEL RIGHT

"Creative problem-solving isn't about showing off," Vaathi says. "It's about solving real problems for real people."

Real Story: IDEO's Shopping Cart Makeover

"IDEO redesigned the shopping cart by talking to shoppers," Vaathi explains. "Their empathy-driven design felt revolutionary."

Pro Tip: Great solutions start with great listening. Stop guessing; start asking.

STEP 7: FAIL BOLDLY—EVERY FAILURE IS DATA

"Failure isn't fatal—it's tuition for success," Vaathi says. "Every wipeout teaches you something new."

Real Story: James Dyson (Again)

"Thousands of failed prototypes weren't setbacks; they were stepping stones," Vaathi adds.

STEP 8: THINK BIG, ACT SMALL

"Big ideas start with small, focused steps," Vaathi explains.

Real Story: Tesla's Sustainable Mission

"Tesla didn't start with solar roofs," Vaathi says. "They began with one luxury electric car. Each small win built momentum."

STEP 9: CREATE WITH ETHICS—BECAUSE IMPACT LASTS LONGER

"Great solutions aren't just effective; they're ethical," Vaathi says.

Real Story: Patagonia's Sustainable Business Model

"Patagonia proves profit and purpose can coexist," Vaathi explains.

Pro Tip: Ask, "Will this solution still matter in 10 years? Will it help more than it harms?"

EXERCISES: PRACTICE YOUR PROBLEM-SOLVING SKILLS

1. Redesign an Everyday Object: Imagine five new uses for a stapler or a spoon.

2. Solve a Ridiculous Problem: How would you stop socks from disappearing in the laundry?

3. Empathy Mapping: Interview someone affected by your challenge and map their thoughts, feelings, and frustrations.

4. Break It to Fix It: Take a broken process and intentionally "destroy" it further to rebuild it better.

CLOSING CHALLENGE: RIDE THE NEXT WAVE

Vaathi leans back, his voice calm but firm. "The waves of life won't stop coming. The choice is yours: flounder or ride with style."

He glances at Kolaru. "Take the problem you've been avoiding, redefine it, and approach it like a surfer—boldly, creatively, and ready to learn from the ride."

Kolaru smirks. "Fine. Let's ride." Vaathi smiles. "Now you're thinking beyond the wave.

WISDOM IN MOTION

SURFING THE OCEAN OF KNOWLEDGE

Have you ever scrolled through memes and felt a curious blend of humor and truth, as if they were whispering secrets about life's deeper realities? What if the wisdom you've been chasing wasn't locked in heavy tomes but hiding in plain sight—wrapped in fleeting moments, a laugh, or a shared nod of recognition?

"Wisdom in memes? Really?" Kolaru muttered, arms crossed. "Next, you'll tell me TikTok holds the secrets to enlightenment."

Vaathi chuckled. "Why not? Wisdom doesn't wear a suit, Kolaru. It hides where you least expect it—like in a child's question, a passing joke, or even a meme. The problem isn't where the wisdom is; it's that we forget to look."

And yet, how often do you find yourself stuck between knowing and doing? The gap between learning and action can feel like trying to surf without a board—thrashing in uncertainty, hoping to catch a wave.

"That gap," Vaathi said, pointing, "is where most people give up. They think knowledge alone is power, but it's not. Applied knowledge is power."

"Sure," Kolaru said with a smirk. "But some things are easier said than done. Like 'letting go.'"

THE CHALLENGE OF LETTING GO

"Ah, letting go," Vaathi mused. "Everyone loves to say it, but doing it? That's where the struggle begins. How do you release what anchors you— old habits, regrets, fears—when your mind clings to them like driftwood in a storm?"

Kolaru raised an eyebrow. "You're saying I should just let go of my fears like flipping a switch?"

"No, not like that," Vaathi replied. "It's not about giving up—it's about finding the freedom to move forward. Letting go isn't a loss. It's lightening your load so you can ride the next wave."

MINDFULNESS IN MOTION

"And then there's mindfulness," Vaathi continued. "We're told it's the answer. But let's be real—who has time to meditate on mountaintops when life feels like a never-ending game of dodgeball?"

"So, what's the alternative?" Kolaru asked.

"Mindfulness isn't about escaping the chaos but about riding it. Learning to stay clear and calm even when everything feels overwhelming. It's not about retreating but thriving right where you are."

THE EDGE OF UNCERTAINTY

"We've all stood at the edge of the unknown," Vaathi said, "facing uncharted waters of uncertainty. It's terrifying, sure—but what if uncertainty wasn't the enemy? What if it's an invitation to explore possibilities you've never dared to imagine?"

Kolaru snorted. "Yeah, sounds poetic. But standing on the edge of the unknown feels more like vertigo than an invitation."

Vaathi smiled. "Only until you take the leap, Kolaru. Uncertainty isn't there to scare you but to stretch you."

BUILDING YOUR OWN COMPASS

"And amid all this noise," Vaathi added, "it's easy to feel lost—like life's currents are dragging you in every direction except the one you want. That's why you need a compass."

"A compass?" Kolaru asked. "You mean some kind of life manual?"

"Not a manual, but a compass forged from your own principles," Vaathi clarified. "One that isn't borrowed from others' expectations but guides you with authenticity and clarity."

WHAT THIS PART IS ABOUT

"This part isn't about prepackaged answers," Vaathi explained. "It's about sparking the right questions—the ones that uncover the wisdom already within you."

"Great," Kolaru said with mock seriousness. "More questions to keep me up at night."

Vaathi smirked. "You'd rather surf without a board? Because that's what life feels like when you stop questioning."

THE RHYTHM OF WISDOM

"Wisdom isn't rigid," Vaathi concluded. "It flows, evolves, and adapts—just like the waves."

"And if you wipe out?" Kolaru asked.

"Then you get back on the board," Vaathi replied with a grin. "Because wisdom in motion isn't about never falling; it's about learning from every ride."

Whether you're savoring life's peaks or bracing against its undertows, these chapters will push you to reflect, challenge assumptions, and discover new perspectives. Together, we'll navigate the tides of modern knowledge—not just to stay afloat but to ride them with purpose, courage, and grace.

"Ready to dive in, Kolaru?" Vaathi asked.

Kolaru grinned. "As long as I don't have to meditate on a mountaintop."

"Good," Vaathi said. "Because the ocean's waiting and the waves are calling."

31

FROM MEMES TO MEANING – TURNING KNOWLEDGE INTO POWER

We're swimming in an endless digital sea where memes, tutorials, and TikTok clips are served faster than our brains can process. It's a double-edged sword: one moment, a meme perfectly captures the absurdity of modern life; the next, a catchy infographic spreads misinformation to millions.

The internet has democratized wisdom, but it's also a weaponized distraction. They say knowledge is power, but here's the catch: knowledge without action is just trivia. It's like owning a Ferrari and never taking it out of the garage. This chapter is about separating the gold from the glitter, applying what matters, and leaving the rest to the void of forgotten bookmarks.

Kolaru crossed his arms, raising an eyebrow. "So, you're saying we're drowning in information?"

Vaathi leaned forward with a knowing look. "Yes, but most people aren't swimming; they're just floating along, letting the waves take them wherever."

SECTION 1: FINDING MEANING IN THE DIGITAL CHAOS

THE MEME ECONOMY: INSIGHTFUL, OVERSIMPLIFIED, AND SOMETIMES MISLEADING

Memes are the digital age's folklore. They distill truths, spark humor, and create instant connections—but they also oversimplify complex ideas.

Example:

- Insightful: A meme about "adulting" hilariously critiques the absurdities of modern responsibility.

- Misleading: A meme twisting statistics to fit an agenda spreads misinformation faster than you can say "context matters."

Vaathi leaned forward with a knowing look. "Memes can be powerful, Kolaru. They make you laugh, think, and connect. But they can also mislead."

Kolaru crossed his arms, raising an eyebrow. "So, what's the solution? Stop laughing at memes? That sounds boring."

Vaathi leaned forward with a knowing look. "No, the solution is to ask questions. Who made it? What's their agenda? Is it satire, or is it serious?"

Pro Tip: Use memes as conversation starters, not as your sole source of truth.

BEYOND MEMES: THE RISE OF DIGITAL EDUTAINMENT

In today's hyperconnected world, platforms like YouTube and TikTok are revolutionizing how we consume knowledge. They've blurred the lines between entertainment and education, giving rise to a new era of digital edutainment. Channels like Tamil Pokkisham, Vyugam, Arasiyal Sadhurangam, and Praveen Mohan have turned the art of storytelling into a medium for learning, bringing history, politics, and science directly to your screen.

Vaathi leaned forward with a knowing look. "Take Praveen Mohan, for instance. His videos delve into ancient mysteries, exploring temples, sculptures, and architectural wonders. Instead of Googling for quick facts, he takes you straight to the stones—showing you history carved into time itself."

Kolaru crossed his arms, raising an eyebrow. "Great! Another channel to binge-watch. But does it actually make me smarter, Vaathi? Or just more distracted?"

Vaathi leaned forward with a knowing look. "Depends on how you use it, Kolaru. Snackable content is a starting point, not a destination. It's what you do with that curiosity that counts."

THE DOUBLE-EDGED SWORD OF SNACKABLE CONTENT

But here's the catch: snack-sized content is like junk food for the brain. Sure, it's easy to consume but often leaves you intellectually hungry. A short video on stoic philosophy can't replace the depth of reading Marcus Aurelius' Meditations. A TikTok on quantum physics might pique your interest but won't make you the next Einstein.

Vaathi leaned forward with a knowing look. "The danger lies in mistaking micro-learning for mastery. The algorithm serves up bites of information, but real understanding requires chewing over ideas, exploring nuances, and turning pages in a book."

Kolaru crossed his arms, raising an eyebrow. "Books again? Come on, Vaathi. Who has the time?"

Vaathi leaned forward with a knowing look. "You have time to scroll endlessly, don't you? Priorities, Kolaru. It's about replacing passive consumption with active learning."

SECTION 2: FROM KNOWING TO DOING – THE ALCHEMY OF ACTION

WHY KNOWLEDGE WITHOUT ACTION IS A LOST OPPORTUNITY

A degree that gathers dust, a tutorial never applied, or an idea abandoned before execution—all represent untapped potential.

Vaathi leaned forward with a knowing look. "So, Kolaru, what do you do with all that knowledge you keep acquiring?"

Kolaru crossed his arms, raising an eyebrow. "What do you mean? I know lots of stuff."

Vaathi leaned forward with a knowing look. "Knowing isn't doing. Do you apply any of it? Or does it sit in your head like an unused tool?"

Kolaru crossed his arms, raising an eyebrow. "Well… I guess it's mostly in my head."

Vaathi leaned forward with a knowing look. "Exactly. A tool that's never used is just wasted potential."

Witty **Insight:** Knowledge without action is like assembling IKEA furniture without the manual—you're stuck with pieces that could have been amazing.

BRIDGING THE KNOWLEDGE-ACTION GAP

The leap from knowing to doing isn't as daunting as it seems. It starts with reframing: stop hoarding information "just in case" and start applying it "just in time."

What Works:

- Elon Musk's Method: Read voraciously, but act immediately—whether it's launching a rocket or designing a car.

- Marie Curie's Genius: Study, experiment, and create impact (hello, portable X-rays).

Kolaru crossed his arms, raising an eyebrow. "Wait, so you're saying I need to build rockets now?"

Vaathi leaned forward with a knowing look. "No, Kolaru. I'm saying stop waiting for perfect conditions. Apply what you know today, even if it's messy."

SECTION 3: STRATEGIES TO BRIDGE THE GAP

1. Start Small and Act Fast. Don't wait for perfect conditions—apply what you know today, even if it's messy.

   Example: Learn three guitar chords. Write a song.

   Vaathi leaned forward with a knowing look. "See, Kolaru? It's about starting small. You don't need to master everything overnight. Just start."

2. Embrace Feedback Loops. Action generates feedback, refining your knowledge in real-time.

   Example: A baker improves by baking and tweaking recipes—not by reading about yeast for years.

   Kolaru crossed his arms, raising an eyebrow. "So, like baking a cake? You must mess up a few times before you get it, right?"

   Vaathi leaned forward with a knowing look. "Exactly. Feedback is your best teacher."

3. Focus on Relevance. Learn what you need now. The rest can wait.

    Pro Tip: Think like JIT (Just-in-Time) manufacturers—only acquire what's immediately useful.

THE CALL TO ACTION

The digital age offers an ocean of knowledge, but it's up to you to turn it into waves of impact.

Mantra: Seek. Learn. Act.

Vaathi leaned forward with a knowing look. "The internet is your surfboard. The memes, videos, and articles—the waves. Your challenge is to paddle out and ride them to meaningful shores."

Ignorance isn't Bliss; It's Expensive

32

THE PRICE OF IGNORANCE

"Ignorance is bliss" may be comforting to say, but it's a lie with expensive consequences. Staying uninformed doesn't protect you from life's complexities; it leaves you vulnerable to them. Whether it's financial illiteracy, ignoring personal growth, or staying silent in the face of societal injustice, ignorance isn't passive—it's a choice, and it costs.

From missed opportunities to costly mistakes, ignorance is a burden that compounds over time. This chapter examines why staying informed is a non-negotiable part of success and provides actionable strategies to escape the traps of ignorance.

SECTION 1: WHY IGNORANCE ISN'T BLISS

1. Missed Opportunities. If you don't know, you can't act. And when you can't act, life's best chances slip away.

    Example:

    o   Finance: Lack of financial literacy can mean missing out on wealth-building opportunities like compound interest or strategic investments.

    o   Relationships: Misunderstanding emotional cues leads to unnecessary conflicts and unresolved issues.

Vaathi tapped the table with a thoughtful expression. "Kolaru, ever heard of compound interest?"

Kolaru shrugged. "Isn't that something banks talk about to confuse us?"

Vaathi chuckled. "No, it's what's making the rich richer while others stay stuck. Ignorance of it is costing people their futures."

2. Vulnerability to Manipulation. Ignorance isn't freedom; it's a leash held by those who exploit your blind spots.

    Example:

    o   Literature: In George Orwell's 1984, "Ignorance is strength" becomes a tool for control, illustrating how ignorance perpetuates oppression.

    o   Reality: Financial scams thrive on the uninformed, preying on their inability to fact-check or recognize red flags.

    Kolaru crossed his arms, raising an eyebrow. "So, you're saying people get scammed because they don't know enough?"

    Vaathi nodded. "Exactly. Scammers count on ignorance. Knowledge isn't just power—it's protection."

    Pro Tip: Knowledge isn't just power—it's protection.

3. The Domino Effect of Ignorance: Ignorance in one area rarely stays contained; it spills into other aspects of life.

    Example:

    o   Neglecting career development can lead to financial instability, strained relationships, and a lack of fulfillment.

    o   Avoiding health knowledge results in preventable illnesses that ripple into work and family life.

    Vaathi leaned forward. "Think about it, Kolaru. One area of ignorance can create ripples. It's never just one missed opportunity."

    Kolaru frowned. "Okay, so what's the solution? Learn everything?"

    Vaathi smirked. "No, start by being curious. Curiosity is the antidote to ignorance."

SECTION 2: POWER DYNAMICS – KNOW THE GAME

Power isn't just for politicians and CEOs—it's everywhere, from boardrooms to friendships. Understanding power dynamics doesn't make you manipulative; it makes you aware.

Important Disclaimer: These principles of power aren't commandments to follow blindly. They are observations of how power tends to work in human interactions. Awareness of these dynamics can protect you from manipulation. Just because these principles exist doesn't mean you have to use them—it's more about recognizing when others might be using them on you.

SIMPLIFIED POWER PRINCIPLES FOR NAVIGATING RELATIONSHIPS

1. Self-Preservation and Defense

   o Stay Aware: Know who holds power in a room and how they wield it. Ignorance of power structures makes you vulnerable.

   o Conceal Intentions: Not every thought needs to be shared. Hold your cards close until the time is right.

   o Avoid Negative Influences: Surround yourself with people who uplift you. Avoid those who constantly bring problems without solutions.

2. Gaining Influence Without Manipulation

   o Adapt to Your Audience: People respond differently to different approaches. Tailor your communication to the person in front of you.

   o Master the Art of Timing: Knowing when to act is often more important than knowing what to do.

   o Inspire Trust: Be reliable and consistent. People follow those they trust.

3. Navigating Risk and Uncertainty

   o Stay Adaptable: Be ready to change course when circumstances shift. Rigidity leads to failure.

   o Focus on What You Can Control: Don't waste energy on things outside your influence.

   o Be Prepared for the Unexpected: Always have a backup plan.

SECTION 3: FINANCIAL IGNORANCE – THE SILENT WEALTH KILLER

Vaathi adjusted his chair. "Now, let's talk about the elephant in the room—finance. Kolaru, how do you manage your money?"

Kolaru scratched his head. "Well… I earn and spend. What's there to manage?"

Vaathi sighed. "That's exactly the problem. Financial ignorance isn't just about not knowing how to invest—it's about not understanding how money works."

KOLARU'S DEBT TRAP

Kolaru leaned back smugly. "You know, Vaathi, I've got it all figured out. I use my credit card for everything and just pay the minimum amount due every month."

Vaathi raised an eyebrow. "And when the limit runs out?"

Kolaru grinned. "I take out a personal loan to pay off the credit card. Then, when that's not enough, I get a top-up loan to cover the new credit card bill. Problem solved!"

Vaathi couldn't help but laugh. "Kolaru, you're not solving problems—you're digging yourself deeper. You've turned debt into a lifestyle!"

Kolaru blinked. "Wait, what's wrong with that?"

Vaathi leaned in. "Do you realize that by the time you get a top-up loan, you've mostly been paying interest for a year without touching the principal? It's like running on a treadmill—lots of effort, but you're going nowhere."

Pro Tip: This cycle of debt is a trap. Here's how to avoid it:

1. Spend Only What You Earn: If you can't pay it off immediately, don't buy it. Credit cards aren't free money but loans with high interest.

2. Live Within Your Means: Ask yourself, "Do I need this, or do I just want it?" Focus on needs before wants.

3. Borrow Only What You Can Repay: Before taking any loan, calculate if you can comfortably manage the monthly repayments without compromising your essentials.

4. Build an Emergency Fund: Avoid using credit for emergencies. Save at least 3-6 months of living expenses to cover unexpected costs.

Vaathi's final word: "Financial discipline isn't about denying yourself—it's about ensuring you don't sacrifice your future for momentary pleasures. And Kolaru, we could write an entire book on debt traps, but for now, stick to these basics."

SECTION 4: POLITICAL IGNORANCE – VOTING BEYOND SURFACE LEVEL

Vaathi leaned back, arms crossed. "Let's talk politics, Kolaru. Who did you vote for in the last election?"

Kolaru smirked. "I voted for the party that my family always supports. Isn't that what everyone does?"

Vaathi shook his head. "And that's exactly the problem. Political ignorance isn't just about not knowing who the candidates are—it's about failing to understand their policies, their track records, and who they really serve."

Why Political Ignorance Is Dangerous:

- Identity Politics: Many people vote based on race, religion, or celebrity endorsements without analyzing the actual policies.

- Media Bias: The media often serves agendas, making it difficult to find unbiased information.

How to Make Informed Voting Decisions:

1. Research Candidates' Policies: Look beyond slogans and promises. Read manifestos and analyze their practicality.

2. Fact-Check News Sources: Use fact-checking websites to verify claims made by politicians.

3. Engage in Local Politics: Attend town hall meetings or follow your local representatives' actions.

4. Discuss with Diverse Groups: Get perspectives from people outside your immediate circle to challenge biases.

Pro Tip: A responsible voter doesn't follow trends; they follow facts.

SECTION 5: TECHNOLOGICAL IGNORANCE – THE DIGITAL DIVIDE

Ignoring technological advancements can leave you behind in a fast-paced world.

Example:

- Cybersecurity Risks: Not understanding basic digital security can make you vulnerable to scams and identity theft.

- Digital Skills Gap: Many people miss out on job opportunities because they lack essential digital skills.

Vaathi: "Technology isn't just for the younger generation, Kolaru. It's a necessity for everyone."

Kolaru: "I guess I need to learn a few things."

Vaathi: "Exactly. Start with cybersecurity basics and build from there."

IGNORANCE IS THE MOST EXPENSIVE CHOICE

Ignorance costs more than money—it costs opportunity, growth, and peace of mind. But combating ignorance doesn't mean knowing everything—it means staying curious, seeking understanding, and acting on what you learn.

Mantra: "Ignorance isn't the absence of knowledge; it's the refusal to seek it. Replace fear of the unknown with a hunger for discovery."

Kolaru (Excuses): "Why even bother at this point? It feels too late."

Vaathi (Truth): "Because if you stop now, everything you've learned goes to waste. Keep moving."

MINDFULNESS FOR REALISTS: RIDING STEADY AMID THE WAVES

THE MYTH OF PERPETUAL CALM

"Mindfulness?" Kolaru snorted. "Isn't that just sitting cross-legged on a mountain, waiting for inner peace to appear magically?"

Vaathi chuckled. "That's the myth: serenity, lotus poses, and perfect calm. But let's be real—life doesn't pause for mindfulness. Deadlines, demanding relationships, and malfunctioning gadgets won't wait for you to 'find your center'."

"So, what's the point, then?" Kolaru asked. "If life's chaos won't stop, why bother?"

"The point," Vaathi said, "isn't to stop the waves—it's to learn how to ride them without getting swept away."

WHAT IS MINDFULNESS, REALLY?

"People think mindfulness is about silencing your thoughts or escaping chaos," Vaathi explained. "But it's not. Mindfulness is about awareness—being fully present and observing your internal and external experiences without judgment."

"Sounds complicated," Kolaru muttered.

"It's not. Think of it like this: mindfulness is your internal weather app. It won't stop the storm, but it will help you prepare."

"So, it's not about calm?" Kolaru asked.

"No," Vaathi replied. "It's about clarity. It's noticing the storm without letting it control you."

PRACTICAL MINDFULNESS TECHNIQUES

"You're saying it's practical?" Kolaru raised an eyebrow.

"Completely practical," Vaathi said. "Here's how you can apply it."

ANCHOR YOURSELF

"When chaos hits, find an anchor to ground you. It could be your breath, a mantra, or even the sensation of your feet on the ground."

"Like what?" Kolaru asked skeptically.

"Imagine you're overwhelmed at work," Vaathi said. "Pause and focus on your breath. Count each inhale and exhale up to ten, then repeat. It's simple but effective."

LABEL THE CHAOS

"Most people say, 'Everything's falling apart!' But that's not helpful," Vaathi continued. "Instead, name the specific emotion you're feeling."

"Why?" Kolaru asked.

"Because naming emotions reduces their power. It shifts your mindset from reactive to reflective."

"So instead of 'My life is a mess,' I say, 'I feel anxious about this deadline?'"

"Exactly."

BREAK DOWN THE WAVES

"Big problems seem insurmountable because we see them as one giant wave," Vaathi said. "Break them into smaller, manageable ripples."

"Like what?" Kolaru asked.

"If the house is a disaster, don't aim to clean everything," Vaathi explained. "Start with one corner of one room."

"Small steps?"

"Exactly."

PRACTICE THE PAUSE

"One of the most powerful tools is the pause," Vaathi continued. "When someone snaps at you, don't react immediately. Take a deep breath. That small pause creates space for a thoughtful response."

"Easier said than done," Kolaru muttered.

"It's a practice," Vaathi said. "The more you do it, the stronger that muscle gets."

CELEBRATE MICRO-WINS

"People focus too much on the big victories," Vaathi said. "But progress often comes in small steps. Acknowledge those moments."

"Like what?"

"Checked one task off your to-do list? Celebrate it. Small wins create a domino effect of positivity."

THE MINDFULNESS MUSCLE

"So, mindfulness isn't a one-time fix?" Kolaru asked.

"No," Vaathi said. "It's a practice. Like any muscle, it grows stronger with consistent use."

"How do I build that muscle?" Kolaru asked.

"Start small. Take five minutes a day to observe your breath. No apps, no distractions—just you and your breath."

WISDOM IN THE WAVES

"Even the most tumultuous ocean has moments of calm," Vaathi said. "Life's chaos, like the waves, is temporary. Mindfulness doesn't erase the waves—it teaches you to ride them with balance."

Kolaru squinted. "Like who?"

"Marcus Aurelius," Vaathi replied. "A Roman Emperor who led during times of war and plague. His meditations reveal how stoic philosophy and mindfulness helped him remain steady."

"So, calm amid chaos is possible?"

"Not just possible—it's powerful."

STEPS TO STAY STEADY

"So, what are the key steps?" Kolaru asked.

"Here's a quick guide," Vaathi said.

1. Anchor Yourself: Focus on something tangible to ground you.
2. Label the Chaos: Name your emotions to regain control.
3. Break Down the Waves: Tackle challenges into manageable pieces.
4. Practice the Pause: Create space between stimulus and response.
5. Celebrate Micro-Wins: Recognize small victories to build momentum.

THE REALIST'S MANTRA

"Life's waves will come," Vaathi said, his voice steady. "But I will ride steady—not because the waves are small, but because my balance is strong."

Kolaru folded his arms. "So, you're saying I don't need to be calm always?"

"Exactly," Vaathi said. "Mindfulness isn't about achieving perpetual calm. It's about staying present, steady, and engaged amid life's storms."

MINDFULNESS FOR THE EVERYDAY SURFER

"Think of life like surfing," Vaathi continued. "You can't stop the waves, but you can learn to ride them."

"Sounds easier than it is," Kolaru muttered.

"Of course," Vaathi replied. "But with practice, you won't just survive the waves—you'll ride them with confidence and grace."

Kolaru sighed. "Why even bother at this point? It feels too late."

Vaathi smiled. "Because if you stop now, everything you've learned goes to waste. Keep moving."

RIDE STEADY AMID LIFE'S WAVES

"So, grab your board," Vaathi said, standing tall. "Find your anchor and ride steady. Life's storms may come, but your balance will keep you afloat."

Kolaru grinned. "Time to ride."

"Exactly," Vaathi said with a knowing smile. "Life doesn't wait for you to be calm. But if you're steady, you'll handle the waves with style."

34 LETTING GO – RELEASING ATTACHMENTS TO STAY AFLOAT

RIDING THE WAVES OF LETTING GO

"Letting go?" Kolaru scoffed. "Sounds like giving up."

Vaathi shook his head. "It's not surrender—it's survival. It's about creating space for new waves, fresh opportunities, and uncharted adventures. Whether it's a grudge, an outdated goal, or a toxic relationship, clinging to what no longer serves you is like gripping a sinking surfboard. The longer you hold on, the faster you sink."

Kolaru frowned. "But it's not easy to let go. It's hard to move on."

"I'm not saying it's easy," Vaathi said. "But it's necessary. Life doesn't wait for you to let go. The waves keep coming, whether you hold on or not."

THE ESSENCE OF LETTING GO

"So, what exactly do you mean by 'letting go'? Isn't it just giving up?" Kolaru asked.

"Letting go isn't giving up," Vaathi explained. "It's growth. Holding on often reflects fear, not strength. Releasing something doesn't mean you've failed—it means you've made space for something better."

Vaathi leaned in. "Imagine trying to surf while holding on to an anchor. The tighter you hold, the faster you sink."

Kolaru chuckled. "Yeah, that sounds like me."

RIDING THROUGH GRIEF AND LOSS

"Letting go of people, dreams, or phases of life isn't easy," Vaathi said. "Grief is a wave, not a straight line."

Kolaru looked away. "I don't want to deal with that."

"I know," Vaathi said softly. "But the only way out is through. Grief ebbs and flows. Feel it, and let it move through you."

They sat quietly for a moment before Vaathi broke the silence.

"Here's something important," Vaathi said. "When someone dies, take your children with you to the grieving family's house."

Kolaru frowned. "What? Isn't that too much for kids?"

"No," Vaathi said. "But here's the thing—it's not just about taking them. It's about talking to them. If you don't explain what's happening, they won't understand anything."

KIDS NEED CONVERSATIONS, NOT JUST EXPOSURE

Vaathi continued, "When I was a kid, my grandfather passed away. The funeral rituals were going on, and some people were beating drums and dancing to give him a stylish send-off. I didn't know what was happening—I thought it was a celebration."

Kolaru chuckled. "So, what did you do?"

"I joined the dance," Vaathi said with a grin. "For 30 minutes, I was dancing at my own grandfather's funeral, completely unaware of what it meant. Then my aunt noticed me. She pulled me aside and said, 'It's your grandfather's funeral. You shouldn't dance.'"

Kolaru laughed. "And did you stop?"

"I stopped, but I didn't understand anything. That's the point. Kids don't process grief the way adults do. If you don't explain what's happening, they'll interpret it in random ways."

WHY CONVERSATIONS MATTER IN GRIEF

"Think about it," Vaathi said. "If a child sees people crying, he'll get confused. If he sees people sitting silently, he'll wonder why. And if no one explains, he'll just create his own stories."

"So, what should parents say?" Kolaru asked.

"Tell them the truth," Vaathi said. "Explain what death is, why people are sad, and why life will keep moving forward. Don't sugarcoat it. Don't hide it. Kids can handle more than we think—they just need the right conversations."

WHAT HAPPENS IN SUICIDE CASES

Vaathi's tone grew more serious. "And if there's a death by suicide in someone's family, it's even more important to take your kids."

Kolaru's eyebrows shot up. "Suicide? Isn't that too heavy for kids?"

"No. It's a reality they need to see. Here's why—when someone dies by suicide, the house isn't filled with crying people. It's filled with angry people. The family isn't mourning—they're scolding the dead. They're saying things like, 'Why did he do this? How could he leave us like this?' It's not the tragedy people imagine. It's confusion, anger, and regret."

Kolaru frowned. "You've seen this happen?"

"Many times," Vaathi said. "And it's the same everywhere. Kids who see this—and more importantly, kids who hear the right conversations during these moments—understand a crucial truth: death doesn't stop the world. Life goes on, and suicide doesn't solve anything. It only leaves behind more pain."

"So, it's not just about taking kids to funerals but about talking to them afterward?"

"Exactly," Vaathi said. "The exposure opens their eyes, but the conversation strengthens them."

GRIEF ISN'T WHAT PEOPLE THINK

Kolaru sat quietly, absorbing this.

"I remember a conversation at work," he finally said. "A colleague's father was seriously ill, and she looked completely drained—barely holding it together. Then, just three days after he passed, she returned to the office. People started gossiping, saying, 'How can she move on so fast?'"

"And what did you think?" Vaathi asked.

"I… I thought it was strange too. It felt cold."

"That's not cold—it's normal," Vaathi explained. "People misunderstand grief. They think it's about mourning endlessly, but it's not. The fear of losing someone often hurts more than the actual loss. Once the loss happens, we realize there's nothing more we can do. We accept it and move on."

Kolaru was silent.

"Think about it," Vaathi continued. "When someone dies, people always say, 'Go somewhere else. Take a break.' Why? Because staying in the house where the person lived makes it harder to move on. Visitors keep coming, crying, and reminding you of the loss. It keeps you stuck."

"So, going back to work helps?" Kolaru asked.

"Yes. At work, nobody sits with you to cry. They give you tasks and deadlines. It forces you to focus on something else. And that's a good thing."

THE REALIST'S INSIGHT: LIFE MOVES ON

"But what about people who judge?" Kolaru asked. "The ones who say, 'She should be grieving longer.'"

Vaathi shrugged. "That's their ignorance speaking. Grief isn't about how long you mourn. It's about finding your way back to life."

"And that colleague… she wasn't wrong?"

"No," Vaathi said firmly. "She was doing what humans have done for centuries—finding strength in routine and normalcy. That's how you move forward."

Kolaru sighed. "So, grief isn't a performance?"

"Exactly. Everyone grieves differently. Some cry for days. Others need to get back to work. There's no right or wrong way to grieve."

THE FINAL LESSON FOR PARENTS

"Remember this," Vaathi said. "When you take your children to a grieving family's house, don't just let them sit there in confusion. Talk to them. Answer their questions. Tell them what death means. Explain that grief is temporary. And show them that life always moves on."

Kolaru nodded slowly. "So, the real strength comes from the conversation?"

"Yes," Vaathi said. "Without that, kids will just be confused. But with the right guidance, they'll grow up stronger—ready to face any storm."

THE SURFER'S GUIDE TO FREEDOM

"Life's waves are unpredictable," Vaathi said. "But clinging to the past only weighs you down. Letting go isn't losing—it's gaining the freedom to ride forward."

Kolaru nodded slowly. "So… trust the tides?"

"Yes," Vaathi said. "Release the anchor, and embrace the open ocean."

LETTING GO DOESN'T MEAN FORGETTING

"So, letting go means forgetting?" Kolaru asked.

"No," Vaathi said. "Letting go isn't about forgetting—it's about freeing yourself from the weight of what you can't change."

Vaathi leaned in. "People hold on to grudges, outdated goals, toxic relationships, and perfectionism. These things pull you under. The sooner you release them; the sooner you'll float."

PRACTICAL TOOLS FOR LETTING GO

"Okay, I'm listening," Kolaru said. "How do I actually let go?"

FORGIVENESS: THE ULTIMATE FREEDOM

"Holding grudges is like drinking poison and expecting the other person to suffer," Vaathi said.

Kolaru frowned. "Forgiveness sounds good in theory, but what if the other person doesn't deserve it?"

"It's not about them," Vaathi replied. "Forgiveness isn't about excusing harm—it's about freeing yourself. When you hold a grudge, you're the one carrying the weight, not them."

Kolaru sighed. "But letting go feels like losing."

"It's not losing," Vaathi said. "It's choosing peace over pain. Nelson Mandela forgave his captors. He chose unity over resentment. That's how you let go."

Vaathi paused for a moment, reflecting. "You know, Asha Bai, one of my first readers, said something that hit me hard. She told me, 'Forgiving others frees us more than it frees them.' And she said it with this look—like it wasn't just an idea. It was a truth she had lived through."

Kolaru blinked. "She's right. The hardest part is realizing we're the ones who need freedom—not them."

"Yes," Vaathi said, his voice steady. "Forgiveness is never about letting someone off the hook. It's about releasing yourself from the poison you carry. That's the ultimate freedom."

DECLUTTER YOUR SPACE, DECLUTTER YOUR MIND

"Physical clutter mirrors mental clutter," Vaathi said. "Start with your surroundings. Clear one corner of your space, and you'll feel the mental shift."

"Marie Kondo's 'Does this spark joy?' isn't just about stuff—it's about your mindset."

ACCEPTANCE IS KEY

"Resistance creates stress. Acceptance creates peace," Vaathi said. "Letting go starts with accepting what is."

"Elizabeth Gilbert found freedom by letting go of control. She embraced life's unpredictability."

THE REALIST'S INSIGHT: LIFE MOVES ON

"The hardest part of letting go," Vaathi said, "is realizing that life moves on—with or without you."

Kolaru sighed. "Why even bother at this point? It feels too late."

"It's never too late," Vaathi said. "If you stop now, everything you've learned goes to waste."

Vaathi gazed at the horizon. "The world moves on. And so will you."

THE SURFER'S GUIDE TO FREEDOM

"Life's waves are unpredictable," Vaathi said. "But clinging to the past only weighs you down. Letting go isn't losing—it's gaining the freedom to ride forward."

Kolaru nodded slowly. "So… trust the tides?"

"Yes," Vaathi said. "Release the anchor, and embrace the open ocean."

FACING THE UNKNOWN – BRAVING LIFE'S UNCHARTED WATERS

35

RIDING INTO THE UNKNOWN

"The unknown?" Kolaru raised an eyebrow. *"That's just a fancy way of saying I'm about to get screwed."*

Vaathi smirked. *"No, it's the waves you haven't ridden yet. The unknown isn't a trap—it's an invitation. It's where new experiences, lessons, and opportunities live."*

Kolaru shook his head. *"But it's terrifying. Fear thrives in uncertainty."*

"That's true," Vaathi admitted. *"Fear feeds on uncertainty, painting the worst-case scenarios in your mind. But courage isn't about eliminating fear—it's about moving forward despite it. The greatest adventures, the biggest breakthroughs, and the most defining moments happen when you brave the unknown."*

SECTION 1: REDEFINING UNCERTAINTY

"What feels like chaos," Vaathi continued, *"is often just a blank canvas. The unknown isn't just uncertainty—it's potential. It's where creativity takes shape, growth happens, and life surprises you."*

Kolaru crossed his arms. *"So… you're saying chaos can be a good thing?"*

"Exactly. The ocean doesn't give you a map—it gives you a wave. You can either freeze up, afraid of falling or paddle forward and ride it."

The unknown **feels overwhelming** because it lacks guarantees. But it's also where the **best opportunities hide**. History proves it: **Amelia Earhart** didn't explore the skies because she knew what lay ahead—she did it for the thrill of discovery. **Greatness isn't built in comfort zones.**

"So courage isn't about being fearless?" Kolaru asked.

"No," Vaathi replied. *"It's about acting even when fear is screaming at you to stop."*

DO IT SCARED

Kolaru hesitated. *"So… just do it scared?"*

"Yes. That's exactly it," Vaathi said. *"Rosa Parks didn't know what would happen when she refused to give up her bus seat. But she stood her ground anyway. Her courage sparked a movement. She didn't wait for fear to disappear—she acted while it was still there."*

We often think **fear must disappear before we take action.** That's a myth. Fear never fully leaves—it's just drowned out by movement.

So next time doubt creeps in, don't wait. Instead, say:

"I'm scared—and I'm doing this anyway."

Because **the unknown isn't your enemy—it's your next great adventure.**

SECTION 2: TOOLS FOR NAVIGATING UNCERTAINTY

"Before you ride the wave, see yourself conquering it. Visualization builds confidence and prepares your mind for action," Vaathi said.

Athletes like Michael Jordan use visualization to prepare for high-pressure moments, creating mental blueprints for success.

"Uncertainty demands preparation," Vaathi said. "Not for every scenario, but for adaptability."

"Okay," Kolaru said. "What's in this surf kit?"

"Your core skills, your support system, and your mental tools."

Your Surf Kit Includes:

- Core Skills: Your unique experience, talents, and resilience.

- Support System: Friends, mentors, or peers who encourage and ground you.

- Mental Tools: Mindfulness, journaling, and techniques to calm your mind when fear strikes.

"Confidence grows when you know you're prepared, even if the ocean throws surprises your way," Vaathi added.

"The unknown can feel overwhelming, like a towering wave," Vaathi said. "Break it into ripples and tackle them one at a time."

Starting a new job? Focus on the first week—learning names and understanding basic processes—before worrying about long-term goals.

SECTION 3: MASTERING THE UNKNOWN THROUGH MINDSET SHIFTS

"Fear thrives on the unknown," Vaathi said. "But curiosity thrives on exploration. Shift your mindset from 'What if I fail?' to 'What can I learn?'"

Elon Musk didn't know if SpaceX would succeed. His mindset? "Failure is an option here. If things are not failing, you are not innovating enough."

Flexibility is your best asset in uncharted waters. Plans will change; waves will shift. Learn to bend without breaking.

Darwin's theory of evolution highlights adaptability as the key to survival—not strength or intelligence.

"Practice adaptability by embracing small, unexpected changes in daily life—like trying a new hobby or taking a different route to work," Vaathi suggested.

SECTION 4: LEVERAGING YOUR INNER STRENGTHS

"You can't control the ocean, but you can master your surfboard," Vaathi said. "In uncertainty, focus on the things within your power: preparation, attitude, and effort."

"You've faced uncertainty before and survived," Vaathi continued. "Let those moments remind you of your resilience."

Think back to your first day at school, your first job, or your first big risk. What did you learn? How did you grow?

SECTION 5: EMBRACING THE ADVENTURE

"The best parts of life often come unplanned," Vaathi said. "Learn to find joy in not knowing what's next."

J.R.R. Tolkien's hobbits didn't know where their journeys would take them, but the magic of their adventure lay in embracing the unknown.

Uncertainty is just a surprise party waiting to happen.

"Each step into the unknown deserves recognition," Vaathi said. "Celebrate the courage it takes to move forward, even when the path is unclear."

Start a "Bravery Jar." Write down every small act of courage you take and drop it in. Over time, you'll see just how fearless you truly are.

SECTION 6: REAL-LIFE STORIES OF NAVIGATING UNCERTAINTY

1. Jacinda Ardern: During the COVID-19 pandemic, Ardern led New Zealand through uncharted territory with empathy, clarity, and decisive action, turning fear into collective trust.

2. Christopher Columbus: Despite the uncertainty, Columbus set sail for the unknown, discovering lands that reshaped history.

3. Serena Williams: Every match begins with uncertainty, but her focus, adaptability, and confidence have made her one of the greatest athletes ever.

THE SURFER'S GUIDE TO THE UNKNOWN

"Facing the unknown is less about conquering it and more about learning to flow with it," Vaathi said. "Trust your instincts, paddle out, and ride the waves as they come. The ocean's beauty lies in its unpredictability, and so does life's."

YOUR COMPASS – LIVING BY YOUR PRINCIPLES

36

THE ANCHOR OF PRINCIPLES

In the vast ocean of life, where waves shift unpredictably and tides pull in every direction, your principles are your compass. They guide you when the horizon blurs, keeping you steady amid storms and chaos.

Principles aren't lofty ideals; they're the keel of your surfboard, grounding your actions and decisions. Living by them requires intention, reflection, and courage—but it's also the most freeing way to navigate life.

SECTION 1: DEFINING YOUR COMPASS

"So, what are principles anyway?" Kolaru asked.

"Principles are your inner truths," Vaathi explained. "They're non-negotiable values that define who you are and how you live. They aren't rules imposed by others but guideposts you choose for yourself."

Without principles, you're like a surfer chasing every wave, only to wipe out repeatedly. They aren't just theories but actions that align with your core beliefs.

"Your compass is personal," Vaathi continued. "Your values aren't universal; they're uniquely yours. Borrowing someone else's compass might lead you to places you don't belong."

Take Warren Buffett, whose principle of simplicity leads him to focus on a few key investments. Contrast that with Elon Musk's principle of relentless innovation, which drives him to juggle multiple groundbreaking projects. Both thrive because they follow their own compass.

"What's the takeaway?" Kolaru asked.

"Define what success means for you," Vaathi said. "Let your principles align with that vision—not society's."

SECTION 2: USING YOUR COMPASS IN DAILY LIFE

"Okay, I get it," Kolaru said. "But how do I use my compass day-to-day?"

"Test your principles in small decisions first," Vaathi said. "Big decisions often feel overwhelming, but they're just the sum of smaller ones. Practice in daily choices to build confidence in your compass."

If integrity is your principle, practice honesty in small moments—like admitting when you've made a mistake at work.

"Aligning small actions with your values makes it easier to navigate life's bigger waves," Vaathi added.

BE CONSISTENT

"Inconsistent principles confuse your direction," Vaathi continued. "They're like a faulty compass that spins in circles."

Kolaru frowned. "So, should I apply my principles everywhere?"

"Yes," Vaathi said. "If kindness is a value, it shouldn't just apply to friends—it should extend to strangers, coworkers, and even critics."

A compass that works only sometimes is as useful as a broken clock; it's right twice a day but wrong the rest of the time.

STAY TRUE, EVEN WHEN IT'S UNPOPULAR

Living by your principles may invite criticism. Standing firm takes courage but also builds respect and trust.

"Think about Rosa Parks," Vaathi said. "Her decision to stay seated wasn't popular, but her unwavering commitment to equality sparked a movement."

"So, integrity is staying true to your compass even when no one else is watching?" Kolaru asked.

"Exactly."

SECTION 3: REFINING YOUR COMPASS

"Can principles change?" Kolaru asked.

"Absolutely," Vaathi said. "Life is dynamic, and your values should grow with it. Principles aren't meant to be rigid; they're adaptable truths that refine over time."

A principle of ambition in your twenties might evolve into a principle of balance in your forties.

Occasionally questioning your principles doesn't weaken them—it strengthens their foundation. In The Subtle Art of Not Giving a F**k, Mark Manson emphasizes questioning deeply held beliefs to ensure they serve your growth and not your ego.

"Reflection is like recalibrating your compass," Vaathi said. "It's essential for staying aligned."

SECTION 4: LIVING YOUR PRINCIPLES

"Principles are visible only through your actions," Vaathi said. "Saying you value honesty means nothing if your behavior suggests otherwise."

Mahatma Gandhi's principle of nonviolence wasn't just a philosophy—it was his daily practice, visible in every protest and decision.

"Teach your principles," Vaathi added. "Your values create ripples that influence others. Sharing them—through actions, words, or mentorship—multiplies their impact."

Satya Nadella transformed Microsoft's culture by leading with empathy and encouraging his team to embrace the same values.

"Start by sharing your principles with those closest to you," Vaathi suggested. "Lead by example, and let them see your compass in action."

SECTION 5: THE FREEDOM OF LETTING PRINCIPLES GUIDE YOU

"Principles aren't constraints; they're the foundation of freedom," Vaathi said. "When your decisions align with your values, you eliminate second-guessing, guilt, and regret. You live with clarity and purpose."

A well-calibrated compass saves you from chasing waves that don't align with your soul.

J.K. Rowling's principle of prioritizing creativity over commercial pressure allowed her to decline lucrative offers that didn't align with her artistic vision.

THE SURFER'S GUIDE TO PRINCIPLES

"In the end, it's not about perfection," Vaathi said. "It's about progress. Living by your compass doesn't mean you won't get lost—it means you'll always find your way back."

Kolaru nodded. "So, I don't have to know everything—just stay true to what I believe?"

"Exactly. Trust your compass, and you'll never lose your way."

LEGACY IN MOTION
(LEAVING MARKS IN THE SAND)

PART 07

Kolaru sat cross-legged on the shore, tracing patterns in the sand. *"Legacy,"* he muttered. *"Why bother? In the end, everyone gets forgotten."*

Vaathi stood nearby, watching the waves. *"Spoken like someone afraid to make a mark."*

Kolaru looked up sharply. *"Afraid? I'm just being realistic. Why should I care about what happens after I'm gone? It's not like I'll be around to see it."*

Vaathi smirked. *"Ah, there it is—the classic excuse. 'Why bother if I won't see the results?' But let me ask you this—would you plant a tree today, knowing you'll never sit under its shade?"*

Kolaru shrugged. *"Depends. Is it worth the effort?"*

"Worth it?" Vaathi's voice hardened. *"You're asking the wrong question. The real question is: Do you want the world to be better because you lived, or worse?"*

Silence stretched between them, broken only by the waves.

Kolaru tossed a pebble into the water, watching the ripples spread. *"So, it's about the ripples?"*

"Exactly," Vaathi said. *"Your choices ripple out, touching lives in ways you'll never see. You don't get to control how far they go, but you do get to decide what kind of ripples you create."*

Kolaru frowned. *"But what if I screw up? What if my ripples cause more harm than good?"*

"Then you own it," Vaathi said, sitting beside him. *"No one's asking for perfection. The question is, what do you do after the screw-up? That's where legacy is built. Do you double down on your mistakes or change the tide?"*

Kolaru crossed his arms. *"Sounds like a lot of pressure."*

"Life is pressure," Vaathi shot back. *"Pretending otherwise doesn't make it disappear. The difference is whether you crumble under it or use it to carve something meaningful."*

Kolaru tilted his head. *"Alright, let's say I buy into this legacy thing. How do I know I'm leaving the right mark?"*

Vaathi leaned in. *"You don't. And that's the point. Legacy isn't about certainty—it's about intention. It's about showing up every day, even when no one's watching. It's about living in a way that, when people look back, they say, 'Because of them, I'm better.'"*

Kolaru sighed, running a hand through his hair. *"What if no one cares? What if it all fades?"*

Vaathi's gaze didn't waver. *"Someone will care. Maybe it's your family, your community, or someone you'll never meet. Your smallest actions can change someone's life in ways you'll never know."*

The waves continued their relentless rhythm, carving patterns into the sand before retreating back to the sea.

"Think about it," Vaathi said. *"After you're gone, people will look for traces of your life—not just to remember you, but to learn. Will they find footprints that uplift and inspire? Or craters left by harm and neglect?"*

Kolaru's gaze softened. *"So, it's about living with intention?"*

"Exactly," Vaathi said. *"Legacy isn't about grand finales. It's about the quiet moments, the choices no one sees, and the impact you make when you think no one's watching."*

Kolaru leaned back, propping himself up on his elbows. *"And what about the mistakes?"*

"They're part of it," Vaathi said, steady. *"Mistakes teach resilience. They show others how to rebuild. Legacy isn't perfection—it's growth. It's honesty."*

Kolaru nodded slowly. *"Alright, Vaathi. Let's leave some footprints worth following."*

Vaathi stood, extending a hand to help him up. *"Good. Because the ocean doesn't wait—and neither does the future."*

They walked toward the water, their footprints marking the sand—temporary, yet impactful. As the waves rose to meet them, the ripples they created stretched far beyond the shore, carrying their legacy into the endless blue.

37

CREATING RIPPLES: LEAVING AN IMPACT THAT LASTS

RIPPLE BY RIPPLE: BUILDING A LEGACY

Kolaru sat by the shoreline, tossing pebbles into the water, watching ripples spread across the surface. "Legacy? Sounds too grand for someone like me."

Vaathi chuckled, adjusting his stance on the sand. "That's your problem right there. You think legacy is reserved for the famous or the extraordinary. It's not."

"Oh, so now you're going to tell me I'm some hidden hero?" Kolaru smirked. "Come on, Vaathi. No one remembers the small stuff."

"Wrong," Vaathi said, pointing at the ripples Kolaru's pebble had made. "See that? Every small action creates waves. You don't need to launch a moon mission or write the next great novel to leave a mark. Sometimes, it's as simple as lending a listening ear, planting a tree, or encouraging someone to dream bigger."

Kolaru sighed. "But how do I know my ripples will matter?"

Vaathi smiled knowingly. "You don't. And that's the beauty of it. The question isn't 'Will I leave a legacy?' It's, 'What kind of legacy am I creating today?'"

THE RIPPLE EFFECT: SMALL ACTIONS, BIG WAVES

Every action you take sets ripples in motion. The way you greet someone, the tone of your words, and the choices you make—they all create waves. Intentional actions amplify this effect, turning small ripples into enduring legacies.

"Intentional actions, huh?" Kolaru raised an eyebrow. "Sounds like a lot of pressure to be perfect all the time."

"Not perfect," Vaathi corrected. "Intentional. There's a difference. It's about being mindful of your impact. Look at Dr. Abdul Kalam. He planted saplings, mentored students, and paused to nurture young minds. Today, those trees provide shade, and his words inspire generations."

"Sounds like he knew exactly what he was doing," Kolaru said, tossing another pebble.

"Maybe. But I bet he didn't sit around wondering if his ripples would be remembered. He just acted with purpose."

Pro Tip: Legacy isn't built on dramatic gestures. It's the outcome of small, consistent actions that reflect your values.

START WITH YOUR SHORELINE

You don't have to change the world overnight. Begin with your immediate circle—your family, friends, or colleagues. Small ripples close to shore travel farther than you might think.

"So, you're saying I should start by fixing my own mess?" Kolaru asked, rubbing his chin.

"Exactly," Vaathi said. "Narayanan Krishnan, a chef from Madurai, began feeding homeless individuals in his community. What started as a small act grew into the Akshaya Trust, which has provided meals to millions."

"Okay, but what if my immediate circle isn't exactly receptive to my 'ripples'?" Kolaru questioned.

Vaathi nodded thoughtfully. "Then you start anyway. Not everyone will notice or appreciate your efforts right away. But those ripples will travel farther than you think."

Pro Tip: Think of your immediate relationships as your shoreline. Nurture those connections and let your actions ripple outward.

KINDNESS: THE SIMPLEST RIPPLE

Kindness is one of the most powerful ripples you can create. It's often dismissed as trivial, but its effects last far longer than you might imagine. A single act of kindness can transform someone's day—and sometimes, their entire outlook on life.

"Kindness is overrated," Kolaru grumbled. "People just take advantage of it."

Vaathi shook his head. "That's your cynicism talking. Babar Ali, once the world's youngest headmaster, began teaching underprivileged children under a tree. His small act of kindness sparked a movement for education and changed countless lives."

"So, what? I should start a school now?" Kolaru scoffed.

"No," Vaathi said with a smile. "Just start by being kind. A compliment, a smile, a helping hand—it doesn't have to be complicated."

Pro Tip: Kindness doesn't need to be complicated. Start with small, genuine gestures such as a compliment, a smile, or a helping hand.

ALIGN YOUR ACTIONS WITH YOUR VALUES

Your legacy is a reflection of your values in action. What you stand for and how you live those principles define the ripples you create.

"So, should I constantly evaluate myself?" Kolaru asked, rolling his eyes.

"Only if you care about the mark you're leaving," Vaathi replied. "Yvon Chouinard, Patagonia's founder, aligned his company with environmental sustainability. By donating profits to climate initiatives, he demonstrated that business success can coexist with ethical responsibility."

"Seems exhausting," Kolaru muttered.

"Only if you're pretending to be something you're not," Vaathi said. "When your actions align with your values, it's effortless."

Pro Tip: Periodically evaluate your actions. Do they reflect your core values, or is it time for a course correction?

REFLECTING ON YOUR RIPPLE TRAIL

Legacy isn't static; it evolves with your actions. Regular reflection ensures your ripples are moving in the direction you intend.

"Reflection again?" Kolaru sighed. "Is this another journaling exercise?"

Vaathi grinned. "Not necessarily. It's about pausing to ask yourself if your actions align with who you want to be. Gandhi did it constantly. His journals reveal a man deeply committed to self-improvement and authenticity."

"Sounds like a lot of self-doubt," Kolaru said.

"Or self-awareness," Vaathi corrected. "Big difference."

Pro Tip: Reflection is the compass that keeps your legacy aligned with your purpose.

MISTAKES CREATE RIPPLES, TOO

Even mistakes can contribute to your legacy—if you own them. Acknowledging and learning from your missteps adds authenticity and depth to the impact you leave behind.

"But what if my mistakes ruin everything?" Kolaru asked, his voice low.

Vaathi placed a hand on his shoulder. "Then you rebuild. Kiran Mazumdar-Shaw faced early failures in her ventures. Instead of hiding them, she turned them into lessons, building Biocon into a global leader in biotechnology."

"So, it's about owning up?"

"Exactly. Mistakes don't define you but refine you."

Pro Tip: Mistakes are part of the journey. They don't define you but refine you.

CLOSING CHALLENGE: THE LASTING RIPPLE

Legacy isn't about monuments or fame—it's about the lives you touch, the doors you open, and the ripples you leave behind. Start creating those ripples today and trust that the ocean will carry them farther than you can imagine.

"Think about it," Vaathi said. "The smallest ripple can become a wave of change. So, what kind of ripples do you want to create?"

Kolaru gazed at the horizon, a newfound determination flickering in his eyes. "Let's make them count."

Vaathi nodded. "Exactly."

TEACHING THE NEXT WAVE: PASSING DOWN KNOWLEDGE AND STRENGTH

38

HANDING DOWN THE LEGACY OF THE WAVES

"Legacy isn't just about the ripples you create—it's about inspiring others to make their own," Vaathi began, watching Kolaru wrestle with his surfboard.

Kolaru sighed, flopping onto the sand. "Great. Another lecture about legacy? I haven't even figured out my own ride yet, and you expect me to teach others?"

Vaathi chuckled. "You don't need to have it all figured out. The best teachers aren't the ones who claim to know everything; they're the ones who show others how to find their own way through the waves."

"So, what? It's not about riding the biggest wave?"

"No," Vaathi said, his voice steady. "It's about helping others paddle out, face the ocean, and carve their unique paths."

TEACH THEM TO SURF, DON'T JUST HAND THEM A SURFBOARD

Handing over solutions without teaching the skills behind them is like giving someone a surfboard without teaching them how to ride. Empowerment comes from guiding, not micromanaging.

"Imagine giving someone a surfboard but never showing them how to balance or read the waves," Vaathi said. "What happens?"

"They wipe out," Kolaru answered.

"Exactly. Teaching isn't about handing over tools but showing how to use them."

Real Story: Dr. A.P.J. Abdul Kalam believed in mentorship through empowerment, encouraging students to think critically rather than spoon-feeding them answers.

Pro Tip: Offer guidance, not guarantees. Inspire action by asking questions that spark thought instead of handing out solutions.

SHARE YOUR MISTAKES: LESSONS THEY CAN BUILD ON

Mistakes are like scars on a surfboard—they tell stories, carry lessons, and showcase resilience. Sharing your wipeouts shows that falling is part of the process.

"Why would anyone want to hear about my failures?" Kolaru asked.

"Because it makes you human," Vaathi replied. "People don't connect with perfection—they connect with authenticity. Your mistakes can be someone else's guideposts."

Real Story: Dhirubhai Ambani openly shared his failures as Reliance Industries grew, teaching his team to embrace risks without fear.

Pro Tip: Balance stories of success with stories of struggle. Vulnerability builds trust and relatability.

ENCOURAGE CURIOSITY: THE FOUNDATION OF EVERY GREAT WAVE

The best surfers are endlessly curious about the ocean; its patterns, secrets, and possibilities. Nurture curiosity by challenging norms and encouraging questions.

"Why must I ask questions if I already know the answers?" Kolaru asked, folding his arms.

Vaathi smiled. "That's the difference between arrogance and wisdom. The wise keep questioning because they know there's always more to learn."

Real Story: Dr. Rukhmabai Raut, India's first practicing female doctor, asked bold questions that led her to break societal barriers and inspire countless women.

Pro Tip: Replace "That's just how it is" with "What do you think?" Curiosity sparks discovery.

LEAD BY DOING: ACTIONS SPEAK LOUDER THAN ADVICE

People learn best by observing. Demonstrate the values, resilience, and determination you hope to instill.

"Why can't I just tell people what to do?" Kolaru asked.

"Because actions speak louder," Vaathi said. "Mahatma Gandhi didn't just talk about nonviolence—he lived it. That's why millions followed him."

Real Story: Mahatma Gandhi's practice of nonviolence was more influential than his words. He inspired millions by embodying his principles.

Pro Tip: Teach through example. Live the values you want others to adopt.

PROVIDE TOOLS, NOT ANSWERS

Answers are fleeting, but tools endure. Equip others with the skills and methods they can use to tackle challenges independently.

"Isn't it faster to just give people the answers?" Kolaru asked, raising an eyebrow.

"Sure. But fast solutions aren't lasting solutions," Vaathi replied. "Give them a process they can rely on, and they'll solve problems long after you're gone."

Real Story: Verghese Kurien didn't just build Amul—he empowered farmers with tools and knowledge, ensuring the cooperative's longevity.

Pro Tip: Teach the process, not just the outcome. Help them build their "surfboard."

TEACH RESILIENCE: RIDING THROUGH THE FALLS

Every surfer falls; it's getting back up that matters. Normalize failure as a step toward growth.

"Failure still stings, though," Kolaru muttered.

"Of course it does," Vaathi agreed. "But every time you get back up, you're stronger. That's resilience."

Real Story: P.V. Sindhu faced setbacks on her path to becoming an Olympic medalist, but her resilience made her victories even sweeter.

Pro Tip: Frame failure as an opportunity, not an endpoint. Celebrate the courage to try.

CELEBRATE THEIR UNIQUE WAVES

The next wave won't look like yours, and that's the point. Celebrate their individuality and the unique paths they carve.

"But what if they make mistakes I wouldn't have made?" Kolaru asked, concerned.

"Let them," Vaathi said. "Their journey isn't supposed to mirror yours. It's about finding their own rhythm."

Real Story: Rabindranath Tagore rejected traditional molds to create his distinct legacy in art and literature. His individuality became his strength.

Pro Tip: Don't impose your vision. Help others find theirs.

STAY OPEN TO LEARNING FROM THEM

Teaching is a two-way street. The next generation has fresh ideas, perspectives, and energy. Stay humble and open to learning from them.

"So, can I learn from them too?" Kolaru asked skeptically.

"Absolutely. Sunderlal Bahuguna, a leader in the Chipko Movement, often said young activists taught him as much as he taught them. It made him a better leader."

Pro Tip: Treat teaching as a dialog, not a lecture.

PASS DOWN STORIES: THE WAVES OF HISTORY

Stories are the invisible currents that shape humanity's course. They carry wisdom, emotions, and lessons across generations—more powerfully than any rulebook or fact sheet ever could.

"Why tell stories when facts are more reliable?" Kolaru asked, his usual skepticism showing.

Vaathi didn't flinch. "Because facts tell you what happened. Stories tell you why it mattered. Stories connect people to meaning. They don't just teach—they inspire."

Vaathi paused, letting the thought settle before driving home the point.

"Think about it. Governments rise and fall, revolutions spark, and movements endure because of stories. People rally behind those they believe in. They follow stories of resilience, of overcoming adversity—not perfection. Nobody cares about a leader born into privilege. They care about the one who struggled, fell, and rose again."

Kolaru scratched his head. "You mean like… underdog stories?"

Vaathi nodded. "Exactly. It's why history remembers the outcasts—the rebels, the misfits, the so-called broken. Their stories resonate because they reflect the human experience. We all face struggles, so we connect with those who have lived through pain and emerged stronger."

Then Vaathi leaned in, delivering the knockout line:

"The cripple, the bastard, the broken—that's who should rule. Because they have a better story."

Kolaru frowned. "Wait, isn't that from Game of Thrones?"

"Yes. Tyrion Lannister said it when deciding who should rule Westeros. It wasn't the strongest or the richest who was chosen—it was the one with a story of survival. Someone who knew what it meant to fall, to be hurt, and to rise again."

Vaathi continued in a firm voice. "That's the heart of leadership: stories of struggle and redemption inspire more loyalty than privilege ever will. People don't follow perfection—they follow authenticity. They follow stories that reflect their own battles."

"So… you're saying stories can shape governments?" Kolaru asked.

"Yes. Stories build kingdoms and topple them. Stories inspire revolutions. And if you want to teach the next generation, you must pass down stories that give them the courage to lead their own battles. That's how legacies endure."

THE SURFER'S LEGACY: EMPOWERING OTHERS TO RIDE

Empowering the next wave isn't about crafting clones of yourself. It's about giving others the courage, tools, and freedom to ride their own waves. Show them how to paddle, balance, and rise again after every fall.

"Think about it," Vaathi said. "The ocean has space for every wave. Which one will you help shape today?"

Kolaru paused, nodding slowly. "I guess it's time to stop hoarding what I've learned and start passing it on."

Vaathi smiled. "Exactly. That's how legacies are built."

Making Values-Based Choices: Navigating Ethical Crossroads

39

THE WAVES OF ETHICS: NAVIGATING LIFE'S CROSSROADS

Kolaru leaned on his surfboard, staring out at the horizon. "Life's just a series of choices, huh? Pick a wave and ride it out. But what if I pick the wrong one?"

Vaathi stood beside him, arms crossed. "There's no perfect wave, Kolaru. But there's a difference between a wave that carries you forward and one that crashes you into the rocks. Your values are your compass. They guide you through ethical crossroads and help you navigate when the waters get rough."

"Values, huh?" Kolaru raised an eyebrow. "Sounds nice in theory, but life's messy. What happens when your values clash with reality?"

"That's when they matter most," Vaathi replied. "Anyone can stick to their principles when it's easy. The real test is when the tide turns against you."

VALUES: YOUR UNWAVERING COMPASS

Your values define who you are, even when no one is watching. They are your internal guideposts, helping you navigate dilemmas and shape decisions that leave a lasting impact.

"But what if my compass is broken?" Kolaru asked, frowning. "What if I'm not sure what my values even are anymore?"

Vaathi knelt down, drawing a circle in the sand. "Start with this: What are the three things you'd never compromise on, no matter what?"

Kolaru thought for a moment. "Honesty, loyalty… and maybe kindness?"

"Good. Now, use them as a checklist," Vaathi said. "When you face a tough decision, ask yourself: Does this align with my core principles?"

Real Story: Malala Yousafzai stood firm in her values of education and equality, even when it risked her life. Her unwavering commitment turned personal adversity into global advocacy.

Pro Tip: Write down your top three values and use them as a checklist for tough decisions. Ask yourself, "Does this align with my core principles?"

ETHICAL CROSSROADS: WHERE SHORTCUTS TEMPT AND LEGACY MATTERS

Life often offers tempting shortcuts—quicker wins, easier paths, or ways to avoid discomfort. But shortcuts rarely build trust or a legacy.

"I'm tired of taking the hard path," Kolaru admitted. "Why not take a shortcut for once?"

Vaathi shook his head. "Because shortcuts often come with hidden costs. Greta Thunberg didn't take the easy path of silence. She stood by her values, even when it was uncomfortable. Her consistent choices created a global ripple effect."

Real Story: Instead of succumbing to pressure, Greta Thunberg amplified her values through consistent climate activism, refusing to take the easy path of silence. Her decisions continue to inspire global movements.

Pro Tip: When faced with shortcuts, pause and project the long-term consequences. Will this decision add to or detract from your integrity?

THE COST OF COMPROMISE: WHY ETHICS MATTER

When it erodes your values, compromise creates cracks that can grow into fissures. It's often invisible at first but can damage trust, relationships, and reputations over time.

Kolaru sighed. "But what if the compromise seems small? Does it really matter?"

"Small cracks become chasms," Vaathi warned. "Look at Enron. It started with small ethical compromises and grew into one of the biggest corporate collapses in history. Every compromise chips away at the trust—yours and others."

Real Story: The Enron scandal began with seemingly small ethical compromises. Over time, it unraveled into one of the biggest corporate collapses in history.

Pro Tip: Before compromising, imagine explaining your decision to someone you deeply admire. Would you still make the same choice?

THE RIPPLE EFFECT: YOUR CHOICES INFLUENCE OTHERS

Every choice you make sends ripples through your environment—your family, team, or community. Your actions model behavior and set the tone for others.

"So, you're saying people are always watching?" Kolaru asked, scratching his head.

"Exactly," Vaathi said. "Jacinda Ardern's leadership during the Christchurch shootings showed empathy and clarity. Her values-driven decisions united a nation and inspired leaders worldwide. Your choices can inspire, too."

Real Story: Jacinda Ardern's values-driven leadership during the Christchurch shootings exemplified empathy and clarity. Her decisions not only united her nation but inspired leaders worldwide.

Pro Tip: Make your values visible through your actions. People respect and emulate consistency.

WHEN YOU FALL SHORT: THE POWER OF OWNING MISTAKES

Ethical living doesn't mean never failing. It means acknowledging mistakes, taking responsibility, and making amends.

"I hate admitting I'm wrong," Kolaru grumbled. "It makes me feel weak."

"Owning your mistakes makes you stronger," Vaathi countered. "Howard Schultz, the former CEO of Starbucks, publicly apologized for racial bias incidents and implemented changes to address them. Accountability restores trust."

Real Story: Howard Schultz, former CEO of Starbucks, publicly apologized for racial bias incidents in his stores and implemented tangible changes, such as bias training. His accountability restored trust.

Pro Tip: Mistakes are part of growth. Apologize, learn, and show your commitment to doing better.

SEEKING CLARITY IN GRAY AREAS

Ethical dilemmas often exist in shades of gray. When in doubt, consult others with diverse perspectives to illuminate blind spots.

"But what if the right choice isn't clear?" Kolaru asked.

"That's when you ask for help," Vaathi said. "The founders of Ben & Jerry's navigated ethical challenges by engaging their team in open dialog. Collaboration brings clarity."

Real Story: Ben & Jerry's founders relied on open dialog with their team to navigate ethical business challenges and ensure their decisions aligned with their mission of environmental and social responsibility.

Pro Tip: Surround yourself with individuals who challenge your thinking and help refine your decisions.

CONSISTENCY: ETHICS AS A DAILY PRACTICE

Ethics isn't a one-time event—it's a practice. Small, daily decisions build the foundation for credibility and integrity over time.

"So, it's about the little things," Kolaru said.

"Exactly," Vaathi replied. "R.K. Narayan's stories consistently reflected his values. His authenticity built a legacy that endures across generations."

Real Story: Though varied, R.K. Narayan's literary works consistently upheld his values of simplicity and universal storytelling. This authenticity built a legacy that endures across generations.

Pro Tip: Start with small, values-driven choices daily. They compound into a habit of ethical living.

MENTORS AND ALLIES: STRENGTHENING YOUR ETHICAL FRAMEWORK

Navigating ethical crossroads becomes easier with a support system of mentors and allies who share your commitment to values.

"How do I find people like that?" Kolaru asked.

"Seek out those who challenge you to improve," Vaathi said. "Ruth Bader Ginsburg credited her mentors for helping her balance ambition with integrity."

Real Story: Ruth Bader Ginsburg credited her mentors and peers for helping her balance ambition with integrity during her trailblazing career in law.

Pro Tip: Build relationships with people who challenge you to grow ethically. Their insights will guide you through life's dilemmas.

SURFING WITH INTEGRITY

"Ethics aren't just guardrails," Vaathi said. "They're the foundation for meaningful impact. They anchor you during storms and amplify the ripples of your legacy."

Kolaru nodded slowly. "So, the next time I face an ethical choice, should I pause, reflect, and trust my compass?"

"Exactly," Vaathi said with a smile. "It may not be the easiest wave to ride, but it will carry you—and those inspired by you—farther than you can imagine."

40 UNDERSTANDING YOUR INFLUENCE: SEEING BEYOND THE IMMEDIATE HORIZON

SURFING BEYOND THE WAVE: YOUR INFLUENCE IN MOTION

"Why do you keep saying I have influence?" Kolaru muttered. "I'm not some leader or celebrity."

Vaathi chuckled. "Influence doesn't require power or fame. It thrives in the everyday. Every word you say, every action you take—it all leaves a mark. Like a pebble tossed into a pond, your presence sends ripples far beyond what you can see."

"So, you're saying I'm tossing pebbles everywhere?" Kolaru asked, skeptical.

"Yes," Vaathi said. "But the real question is—are those ripples helping or hurting? Are they inspiring or destroying?"

Kolaru fell silent, realizing that even inaction was a ripple.

INFLUENCE: THE RIPPLE YOU CONTROL

Ignoring your influence is like paddling through the ocean without realizing the current you create. Whether you're a parent, a teacher, a friend, or a leader, your actions ripple outward—whether intentional or not.

"People underestimate the ripples they create," Vaathi continued. "They think their actions end in the moment. But ripples travel farther than we realize."

Real Story: The Silent Ripple of Field Marshal Sam Manekshaw

Sam Manekshaw, India's first Field Marshal, wasn't known for grand speeches but for his calm, decisive leadership during critical moments like the 1971 Indo-Pak war. His quiet confidence and strategic thinking created ripples that inspired trust and respect across ranks.

"He didn't need to shout or boast," Vaathi said. "His influence was in his calm presence, strategic thinking, and quiet resilience."

Pro Tip: Ask Yourself—What Ripple Are You Creating Today?

Your daily actions shape your influence. Choose them wisely.

THE BUILDING BLOCKS OF INFLUENCE

1. YOUR WORDS ARE WAVES

Words have a long shelf life. They can uplift, inspire, and unite, or they can alienate and divide.

"You think words disappear once they're spoken?" Vaathi asked. "They don't. They echo long after you've left the room."

Example: The Visionary Words of Ignaz Semmelweis

Dr. Ignaz Semmelweis, a 19th-century Hungarian physician, used his influence to advocate for handwashing in hospitals, saving countless lives despite resistance from his peers. His persistence with simple, impactful words eventually transformed global medical practices.

2. PRESENCE SPEAKS LOUDER THAN WORDS

Sometimes, your influence lies not in what you say but in how you show up. Being fully engaged and authentic creates trust and leaves a lasting impression.

"People can smell fake from a mile away," Vaathi said. "If you're not authentic, your influence fades before it even begins."

Example: The Leadership of Mary Parker Follett

A pioneering management thinker, Follett championed collaboration and respectful leadership long before they were corporate buzzwords. Her ability to be present and engage deeply with diverse viewpoints continues to influence organizational practices today.

3. CONSISTENCY BUILDS TRUST

Your influence is strongest when you're reliable. People trust those who consistently align their actions with their words.

"Trust is a slow build," Vaathi said. "But it crumbles instantly if your actions don't match your words."

Example: The Steady Hand of Masaru Ibuka

Masaru Ibuka, co-founder of Sony, consistently demonstrated a commitment to innovation and quality. His leadership inspired the trust and loyalty of employees and customers alike, helping to build Sony into a global brand.

EMPATHY AND HUMILITY: QUIET PILLARS OF INFLUENCE

"Why does everyone talk about empathy these days?" Kolaru asked. "Isn't it just another corporate buzzword?"

Vaathi shook his head. "Empathy isn't a trend. It's what makes influence stick. People don't follow leaders who preach—they follow leaders who listen."

Example: The Humble Influence of Dr. Devi Shetty

Dr. Devi Shetty, a renowned cardiac surgeon and philanthropist, revolutionized affordable healthcare in India. His empathetic approach to patients and humility in service have rippled across communities, inspiring a new era of medical accessibility.

THE RIPPLE EFFECT OF UNINTENTIONAL INFLUENCE

"Even when you're not trying, you're creating ripples," Vaathi said. "How you treat others, handle challenges, or celebrate success leaves a lasting impact."

Kolaru scratched his head. "So even my silence is a ripple?"

"Yes. Silence speaks too. The way you don't act also influences people."

Example: The Unseen Influence of Isamu Noguchi

A Japanese-American artist, Isamu Noguchi, quietly reshaped public spaces with his designs. His work influenced aesthetics and how people experience community and harmony in shared environments.

EMPOWERING OTHERS: THE MULTIPLIER EFFECT

True influence isn't about control but empowering others to lead. When you inspire someone to find their own strength, your ripple effect multiplies exponentially.

"Think about it," Vaathi said. "When you teach someone to surf, they don't just catch waves for themselves—they inspire others to paddle out too."

Example: Kailash Satyarthi's Empowerment Movement

Nobel laureate Kailash Satyarthi's work to end child labor isn't just about rescue—it's about empowering children and communities to resist exploitation. His ripple effect continues to grow through the lives he's touched.

CLOSING CHALLENGE: SEEING BEYOND YOUR WAVE

Kolaru shook his head. "But why even bother? It feels like it's too late to make an impact."

Vaathi's gaze was steady. "Because if you stop now, everything you've learned goes to waste."

He leaned in closer. "The thing about influence is—you may never see where your ripples end. But that doesn't mean they don't exist. Your influence doesn't end with you. It travels farther than you can imagine."

Vaathi's voice softened. "Every time you show up, every time you choose kindness or courage, you're creating ripples that will outlast you."

RIDE WITH PURPOSE: SURFING THE WAVES OF INFLUENCE

Your influence is your surfboard; it's how you navigate life's waves and guide others along the way. By acting with intention, leading with humility, and empowering those around you, you can create ripples that inspire waves of change far beyond your horizon.

Vaathi stood gazing at the ocean. "So, what ripple will you create today?"

Kolaru paused, looking out at the horizon. "I guess it's time to stop complaining and start paddling."

"Exactly," Vaathi said with a knowing smile. "Ride the wave with purpose—and trust that your influence will carry farther than you ever imagined."

BLUEPRINTS OF SUCCESS: FOLLOWING THE PATH OF TRAILBLAZERS

EVERY GREAT LEGACY BEGINS WITH A CHOICE

"Have you ever wondered what separates ordinary people from trailblazers?" Vaathi asked, watching Kolaru doodle aimlessly in the sand.

Kolaru shrugged. "Luck, probably. Right place, right time."

Vaathi shook his head. "It's a choice. Every great legacy begins with a choice."

With a quick swipe of his finger in the sand, Vaathi drew a line. "Comfort on one side. Challenge on the other. Which side do you think trailblazers choose?"

Kolaru smirked. "Challenge. But that's easy to say when you're not standing at the edge of the abyss."

"True," Vaathi agreed. "But the difference is—trailblazers see the abyss and jump anyway. Not because they want fame or fortune, but because they want to make ripples that last."

THE CHOICE OF ACHILLES: GLORY OR OBSCURITY

"Take Achilles," Vaathi continued. "His mother gave him a choice: Stay home, live in peace, and be forgotten. Or go to Troy, face unimaginable challenges, and be remembered forever."

Kolaru rolled his eyes. "Ah yes, the ancient 'go big or go home' speech."

"Except this wasn't just about 'going big.' It was about creating significance. Achilles chose to fight, knowing he wouldn't return. Thousands of years later, his name still echoes across history."

Vaathi paused. "Trailblazers aren't remembered for what they owned or who they were. They're remembered for what they dared to do."

TRAILBLAZERS CREATE RIPPLES THAT LAST

"But greatness isn't reserved for mythical heroes," Vaathi continued. "Trailblazers exist in every era—ordinary people who dare to challenge the tides and build something extraordinary. They make choices that send ripples far beyond what they can see."

Kolaru glanced at the ocean. "So, it's about creating ripples, huh? I thought it was about making waves."

Vaathi grinned. "Ripples become waves. But they start with a single choice."

"Think about Kailash Satyarthi," Vaathi added. "He didn't just rescue thousands of children from forced labor—he sparked a global movement for children's rights. His ripples continue to spread."

COURAGE IN CHOICE: A TRAILBLAZER'S FIRST STEP

"Okay, fine," Kolaru said, leaning in. "So, where does it start? How do you become a trailblazer?"

"Courage," Vaathi said simply. "Trailblazers start with the courage to step into the unknown. Courage isn't the absence of fear—it's the decision to act despite fear."

Vaathi's eyes softened. "My father's letters always began with the words Thunivae Thunai—'Courage is my companion.' It wasn't just poetic. It was a reminder that courage is the currency of progress."

When faced with fear, remind yourself: The waves may be daunting, but the shore you'll reach makes the ride worthwhile.

SUCCESS VS. SIGNIFICANCE: WHAT ARE YOU BUILDING?

"Okay, so let's say I muster some courage," Kolaru said. "Then what? Success?"

"Not quite," Vaathi replied. "Trailblazers know that success is fleeting. What matters is significance."

"What's the difference?"

"Success gets you applause. Significance earns you gratitude," Vaathi explained. "Pharaohs built pyramids to immortalize their names. But most of their names are forgotten. Meanwhile, people like Jane Goodall are remembered for their contributions to conservation and compassion."

"So… significance is about making a real impact?" Kolaru asked.

"Exactly. It's about creating ripples that benefit others, not just yourself."

BUILDING BEYOND THE SELF

"Trailblazers don't just achieve personal success," Vaathi said. "They build systems that empower others."

"Like teachers?" Kolaru asked.

"Yes," Vaathi nodded. "A teacher who inspires students to think critically creates a ripple effect that spans generations. They don't just pass down knowledge—they pass down power."

Ask yourself: "How can I empower others to thrive without me?" True leadership is measured by the success of those you uplift.

LEGACY VS. PERFECTION

"What if I mess up?" Kolaru asked. "Doesn't failure ruin the legacy?"

"Not at all," Vaathi said. "Trailblazers stumble and fail like everyone else. But they embrace their imperfections as part of the journey."

Vaathi smiled. "Steve Jobs was ousted from Apple. That failure didn't define him—his comeback did."

Your failures don't diminish your legacy; they humanize it. They inspire others to persist through their own challenges.

AUTHENTICITY AND PURPOSE: THE CORE OF EVERY TRAILBLAZER

"The most important thing," Vaathi said, "is to live authentically. Trailblazers don't chase trends or popularity. They follow their purpose."

"Isn't that risky?" Kolaru asked.

"Of course," Vaathi replied. "But purpose-driven people aren't interested in fleeting recognition. They want lasting impact."

THE ILLUSION OF IMMORTALITY

"People worry too much about being remembered," Vaathi said. "But social media profiles and accolades will fade. What endures is the work you leave behind."

Vaathi pointed to the horizon. "Think of Rosalind Franklin. Her discoveries laid the foundation for DNA research. Her name might not be as prominent, but her contributions transformed science forever."

Let go of the need to be remembered. Focus on the work, and your legacy will take care of itself.

WRITE YOUR LEGACY IN ACTIONS

"If you're unsure about your legacy," Vaathi said, "try this—write your eulogy. What do you want people to say about you? More importantly, how do you want them to feel?"

Kolaru raised an eyebrow. "You want me to write my own eulogy?"

"Yes," Vaathi said firmly. "Use it to guide your actions today."

RIDE WITH BOLDNESS

"Trailblazers don't follow the waves—they create them," Vaathi said, standing tall.

Kolaru looked out at the ocean. "So, what ripple will I create today?"

Vaathi smiled. "That's up to you. But remember—your legacy isn't a destination. It's a journey shaped by every choice you make."

LEAVING YOUR MARK: BUILDING A LEGACY WITH STYLE

42

(Craft a signature legacy that inspires others to follow your lead.)

LEGACY: A STORY TOLD IN RIPPLES

"Why do people obsess over legacy?" Kolaru asked, frowning. "Isn't it just another way of saying, 'I want to be remembered forever'?"

Vaathi chuckled. "Legacy isn't about being remembered—it's about what is remembered. It's the story you leave behind, whether people know your name or not."

Kolaru scratched his head. "So, it's not about money or titles?"

"No," Vaathi said firmly. "It's about the impact you make. The ripple effect of how you lived, the values you upheld, and how you navigated the waves of life."

Kolaru sat back. "And what makes a legacy stylish?"

Vaathi smiled. "Style isn't about loudness or grandeur. It's about authenticity. A stylish legacy resonates because it's real, unique, and meaningful. It's not the size of your actions, but the way they reflect your essence that leaves a lasting mark."

STYLE IS AUTHENTICITY IN ACTION

"Think of Maya Angelou," Vaathi said. "She didn't just leave behind poetry—she left behind a legacy of courage, empathy, and unwavering commitment to justice. Her words inspired generations to rise above adversity and claim their own voice."

"So, authenticity is the key to a stylish legacy?" Kolaru asked.

"Yes," Vaathi nodded. "Ask yourself: Are you living a life true to your values, or are you chasing someone else's expectations?"

Kolaru looked thoughtful. "Most people are just trying to survive, not think about legacy."

"Exactly," Vaathi said. "Which is why those who live with intention stand out, even in small ways. That's style."

THE BUILDING BLOCKS OF A STYLISH LEGACY

Your Values: The Foundation of Impact

"Values are your compass," Vaathi said. "Without them, your legacy risks becoming scattered and hollow."

Kolaru nodded. "Like those corporate slogans that mean nothing?"

"Exactly," Vaathi said. "Take Wangari Maathai. She founded the Green Belt Movement in Kenya, combining environmental conservation with women's empowerment. Her legacy wasn't about her name but about her values of sustainability and equality, which created ripples felt worldwide."

Consistency: The Subtle Power of Showing Up

"A legacy isn't built in one bold moment," Vaathi said. "It grows from the small, consistent ways you show up."

"Kind of like Fred Rogers?" Kolaru asked. "That guy from Mister Rogers' Neighborhood?"

"Yes," Vaathi said, smiling. "He didn't revolutionize television with flash or grandeur. His quiet consistency, showing up for children every day with kindness and understanding, made him an icon."

Kolaru grinned. "So, being stylish isn't about big gestures. It's about the little things you do every day?"

"Exactly," Vaathi said. "It's about showing up."

Ambition Meets Humility

"Ambition drives innovation," Vaathi continued, "but humility builds trust. Together, they create a legacy that endures."

"Like Ruth Bader Ginsburg," Kolaru said, catching on. "She fought for gender equality but still made meaningful connections with people who disagreed."

"Perfect example," Vaathi said. "She balanced ambition with humility. That's why her legacy isn't just in the courtroom—it's in people's hearts."

Vaathi paused. "Celebrate your wins, Kolaru. But never forget the lessons you still need to learn."

CONNECTIONS: AMPLIFYING YOUR RIPPLE EFFECT

"No one builds a legacy alone," Vaathi said. "It grows through the connections you nurture and the lives you touch."

"Kind of like Harish Hande?" Kolaru asked. "The guy who provided sustainable energy solutions to rural communities?"

"Yes," Vaathi said. "He focused on empowering others to uplift themselves. His legacy isn't in his personal achievements—it's in the communities he transformed."

"So, mentoring is a stylish move?" Kolaru asked.

"It's the stylish move," Vaathi said. "A shared legacy has a greater reach than an individual one."

LEAVE SPACES BETTER THAN YOU FOUND THEM

"Legacy isn't just about achievements," Vaathi said. "It's about the impact you leave on every space and relationship you touch."

"Like Princess Diana," Kolaru offered. "She wasn't just about royal appearances—she worked with marginalized communities and made real improvements wherever she went."

"Exactly," Vaathi agreed. "The true legacy is leaving spaces better than you found them."

REFLECTION AND EVOLUTION: A LEGACY IN PROGRESS

"Legacy isn't static," Vaathi continued. "It evolves as you grow. Reflect on your actions and adapt to new challenges to ensure your impact remains meaningful."

Kolaru frowned. "So, you're saying I can't plan my legacy in advance?"

"No," Vaathi said with a smile. "But you can guide it by staying true to your values and being willing to grow."

"Like Ada Lovelace," Vaathi added. "The world's first computer programmer. Her legacy grew over time as technology evolved. Even though her contributions were underappreciated during her life, today she's celebrated as a visionary."

CLOSING CHALLENGE: LIVE YOUR LEGACY NOW

"So, legacy isn't something you create at the end?" Kolaru asked.

"No," Vaathi said. "It's the culmination of how you live every moment. Your decisions, conversations, and actions today are already shaping the ripples you'll leave behind."

Kolaru looked out at the ocean, watching the waves. "I guess that means I'm already leaving a legacy—whether I realize it or not."

"Exactly," Vaathi said. "The question is—what kind of legacy are you creating?"

SURFING INTO TOMORROW

"Your legacy isn't a destination—it's the waves you create through every intentional action," Vaathi said.

Kolaru stood, brushing off the sand. "So, what ripple do I create next?"

"That's up to you," Vaathi replied with a knowing smile. "But remember—every choice shapes your story. Are you ready to leave your mark with style?"

Kolaru grinned. "Let's surf into the infinite blue together."

SURFING INTO TOMORROW

(THE ENDLESS HORIZON)

The horizon stretches infinitely before you, its hues shimmering with untapped potential. Every wave brings a fresh opportunity; every ripple, a quiet beckoning toward adventure. As the tides of yesterday's retreat leave imprints of wisdom etched into the sands of experience—lessons to carry forward on your next ride.

But the future? The future is an uncharted ocean—vast, untamed, and brimming with mysteries that dare you to explore. It doesn't come with a map, only the promise of transformation. The question isn't what lies ahead—it's how you choose to meet it.

"Let's be honest," Vaathi said, leaning on his board. "Most people stand at the shore, waiting for perfect conditions. But perfection never comes."

Kolaru scoffed. "Easy for you to say. You always act like you have it all figured out."

Vaathi's eyes narrowed. "Figured out? No. But I've stopped waiting for certainty. It's not about knowing every twist of the wave. It's about trusting you'll adjust mid-ride."

"So, what's your secret?" Kolaru asked, curiosity finally breaking through his sarcasm.

"There's no secret," Vaathi replied. "Just this—stop fighting the ocean. Flow with it. Adapt. Innovate. And most importantly—get on the damn board."

Every wave brings a choice. Will you linger at the shore, overwhelmed by the unpredictability of the waves? Or will you paddle out with boldness, ready to carve a unique path through waters no one has navigated before? This isn't about controlling the ocean; it's about trusting yourself—your resilience, intuition, and readiness to adapt—as you embrace its boundless possibilities.

"I've seen too many people drown in their own hesitation," Vaathi continued. "They think playing it safe will protect them. But in reality, standing still is the biggest risk of all."

Kolaru crossed his arms. "And what if I wipe out?"

Vaathi smirked. "Then you wipe out. But at least you'll know you tried. And when you get back up, you'll be stronger, faster, and more prepared for the next wave. Or do you prefer staying on the shore, blaming the tides for never changing?"

The horizon is not a boundary; it's an invitation. It whispers of reinvention, innovation, and growth, daring you to ride the currents of change with grace and intention. Each wave offers a chance to redefine yourself, to challenge conventions, and to craft something breathtakingly original.

Kolaru sighed, running a hand through his hair. "Okay, okay. Let's say I'm ready to paddle out. What if the waves are bigger than I expected?"

"They will be," Vaathi said without hesitation. "Count on it. The question isn't whether the waves will challenge you—it's whether you'll rise to meet them. So, are you ready to stop talking and start riding?"

Kolaru grinned, a spark of determination flickering in his eyes. "Let's do this."

As we enter this final chapter, we shift our gaze forward—not with hesitation, but with exhilaration. This is where legacy transforms into evolution, where yesterday's reflections fuel tomorrow's bold decisions. Here, we realize endings are not finales but preludes to what lies ahead. The ocean, like life, is ever-changing, offering endless opportunities to rise, fall, and rise again with renewed purpose.

"Legacy isn't about what you leave behind," Vaathi said. "It's about what you set in motion. Waves don't stop at the shore—they ripple outward, creating new possibilities beyond what you can see."

"So, you're saying my actions today create tomorrow's waves?" Kolaru asked.

"Exactly," Vaathi replied. "The future isn't a destination. It's a consequence of what you choose to do right now."

Part VIII isn't just about dreaming of the future but shaping it. It's about stepping into the unknown with conviction, creating ripples of change, and leaving space for serendipity to surprise you. Whether your journey takes you toward personal reinvention, professional innovation, or uncharted horizons, this is your moment to paddle out and embrace what's next.

Take a deep breath. Feel the rhythm of the ocean beneath you. The waves are rising, the horizon is calling, and your board is ready. This is the ride of a lifetime—into the endless tomorrow, where every wave promises a new beginning.

"Ready or not, the waves are here," Vaathi said, a gleam of challenge in his eyes. "The only question is—are you?"

Kolaru adjusted his stance, eyes locked on the horizon. "I'm ready."

Vaathi chuckled. "Good. Then let's ride."

43 ADAPTING TO CHANGE – RIDING THE WAVES OF THE FUTURE

Change is the ocean we all navigate—vast, relentless, and unpredictable. No matter how skilled a surfer you are, you cannot control the waves, only how you ride them. You can resist, exhausting yourself by fighting the tide, or you can learn to embrace its rhythm, riding with grace and purpose.

To adapt is not to surrender—it's to evolve. It's about finding balance in uncertainty and trusting your ability to thrive, even when the waters shift beneath you. This chapter explores the art of turning change into an ally, creating opportunities for growth, learning, and reinvention.

RESISTANCE VS. RIDING: CHOOSE WISELY

Resisting change is like paddling against the current—it drains energy without progress. Flowing with the wave allows you to channel your energy into forward motion.

"I don't like change," Kolaru grumbled. "Why fix what isn't broken?"

"Because if you wait until something's broken, you're already too late," Vaathi countered, arms crossed. "Adapt before you're forced to."

Real Story: Kodak's Missed Wave

Despite inventing the first digital camera, Kodak resisted the shift to digital photography. Their reluctance to embrace the tide of innovation led to their decline, proving that staying still in a changing ocean is the riskiest move of all.

Pro Tip: When you feel resistance, ask yourself: "What's the worst that could happen if I try this new approach?"

Exercise: Reflect on a decision where the timing was off and strategize a better timing for future decisions.

FLEXIBILITY: THE SECRET TO STAYING AFLOAT

Adaptability isn't abandoning who you are—it's bending without breaking. Flexibility helps you stay upright, even when the waves grow choppy.

"But what if I lose myself in the process?" Kolaru asked, narrowing his eyes.

"You won't," Vaathi replied. "Adaptability doesn't mean losing your essence—it means strengthening it in new contexts."

Real Story: Netflix's Pivot

Netflix began as a DVD rental service. By pivoting to streaming at the right moment, it not only survived but became a leader in the digital entertainment space.

Pro Tip: Say "yes" to one new idea or challenge each week, even if it feels uncomfortable.

Exercise: Reflect on a decision where the timing was off and strategize a better timing for future decisions.

BUILDING YOUR ADAPTABILITY MUSCLE

Adaptability isn't innate—it's a skill you develop through practice. Like a muscle, it grows stronger the more you stretch it.

"But what if I fail?" Kolaru muttered, tapping his foot nervously.

Vaathi leaned in, voice steady. "Failure is a wipeout. But every surfer knows you get back on the board and learn from it. The only true failure is refusing to adapt."

Real Story: The COVID-19 Pivot

During the pandemic, businesses pivoted overnight—restaurants shifted to delivery, schools embraced online learning, and millions adapted to remote work. Those who evolved quickly thrived in a changing landscape.

Pro Tip: Start with small changes. Try a new routine or approach a problem differently to build your adaptability.

Exercise: Reflect on a decision where the timing was off and strategize a better timing for future decisions.

EMBRACING TECHNOLOGY: RIDING THE NEXT WAVE

Technology isn't the enemy of tradition; it's the vehicle of progress. Embracing it ensures you stay relevant in a rapidly evolving world.

"Technology changes too fast. How can anyone keep up?" Kolaru asked, throwing his hands up.

"By staying curious," Vaathi said. "You don't need to master every new gadget. Just understand the trends and how they impact your life."

Real Story: Tesla's Electric Revolution

Elon Musk's Tesla redefined the automotive industry by embracing electric technology and challenging traditional norms, proving that innovation can disrupt and lead.

Pro Tip: Stay curious about emerging technologies. Even understanding them helps you stay ahead.

Exercise: Reflect on a decision where the timing was off and strategize a better timing for future decisions.

ANCHORING IN YOUR VALUES

Adaptability doesn't mean losing yourself. Your values are the compass that guides you through change, ensuring that you evolve without losing authenticity.

"But what if I have to compromise my values to adapt?" Kolaru asked, his voice tinged with doubt.

Vaathi shook his head. "True adaptability means finding ways to innovate without compromising what matters most."

Real Story: Dr. Abdul Kalam's Legacy

As a scientist, leader, and mentor, Dr. Kalam adapted to the changing needs of his roles while staying steadfast in his values of integrity and education.

Pro Tip: When facing change, ask yourself: "Does this align with my core values?"

Exercise: Reflect on a decision where the timing was off and strategize a better timing for future decisions.

CELEBRATE SMALL PROGRESS

Big changes can feel overwhelming, but small victories build momentum. Celebrate every small step—it's proof of your adaptability and growth.

"Progress feels slow," Kolaru sighed.

Vaathi smirked. "Slow progress is still progress. Even the tiniest ripple can create a wave if you keep at it."

Real Story: India's Mars Orbiter Mission (MOM)

Despite budget constraints, ISRO achieved one of the most cost-effective Mars missions by focusing on incremental progress. Each small step paved the way for monumental success.

Pro Tip: After adapting to a new situation, take a moment to acknowledge what you've accomplished.

Exercise: Reflect on a decision where the timing was off and strategize a better timing for future decisions.

CLOSING CHALLENGE: SURF THE FUTURE

The waves of change aren't slowing down; they're intensifying. The question isn't whether you can stop them; it's whether you'll rise to meet them. The future belongs to those who paddle out boldly, adapting not by abandoning themselves but by evolving with intention and resilience.

"Think of it this way," Vaathi said. "Every wave you ride makes you stronger for the next. The ocean of change is calling—will you ride it or let it drown you?"

Kolaru grinned, his eyes gleaming with determination. "Let's surf."

RIDE THE WAVE

The future is an endless horizon of waves—some calm, some turbulent, but all full of potential. Adapting isn't about mere survival; it's about thriving, learning, and finding joy in the journey. So, paddle out, trust your instincts, and ride every wave with confidence.

The ocean of change is calling: Are you ready to surf?

BALANCING TECHNOLOGY AND HUMANITY – STAYING GROUNDED IN THE DIGITAL AGE

44

Technology is a powerful surfboard in today's interconnected world—amplifying your ability to navigate life's waves. But here's the trick: the surfboard doesn't control the ride; you do.

The digital age offers immense possibilities—instant communication, boundless learning, and tools to amplify creativity. Yet, it also comes with risks: addiction, disconnection, and a loss of authentic human connection. Staying balanced in this landscape requires intentionality—using technology as a tool to enhance life, not overwhelm it.

This chapter explores how to thrive in the digital world by blending innovation with humanity. Let's learn to surf the digital tide without losing touch with our essence.

SET BOUNDARIES: CONTROL YOUR RIDE

"Why does it feel like my phone controls me more than I control it?" Kolaru muttered.

"Because you've handed it the reins," Vaathi replied sharply. "It's time to take them back."

Technology, without limits, can dominate your time and energy. Setting boundaries helps you maintain focus and peace of mind.

Real Story: Bill Gates' Screen-Free Time

Bill Gates prioritizes screen-free family time, demonstrating that even tech pioneers value unplugging to nurture real-world relationships.

Pro Tip: Establish "tech-free zones" at home or commit to screen breaks during meals or before bed.

Exercise: Identify one tech-free zone or time period you can implement this week.

BALANCE SCREEN TIME WITH FACETIME

"Why meet people in person when I can just text?" Kolaru shrugged.

Vaathi shot him a look. "Because texting won't tell you what's behind their eyes or the warmth in their voice. Trust isn't built through screens."

While technology enables connection, it can never replace the depth of in-person interactions. Nurture your relationships offline as much as online.

Real Story: The Power of Face-to-Face Connections

Leaders like Sheryl Sandberg emphasize the importance of personal interactions in building trust and collaboration.

Pro Tip: For every hour spent online, dedicate an equal amount of time to nurturing offline connections.

Exercise: Schedule one face-to-face meeting this week—a coffee with a friend or a family dinner without screens.

USE TECH MINDFULLY: BE INTENTIONAL

"I scroll for hours and still feel empty," Kolaru admitted.

"That's because you're consuming mindlessly," Vaathi said. "Use tech with purpose—not as a distraction."

Technology should enhance productivity and creativity—not distract or overwhelm. Use digital tools with purpose.

Real Story: Mindful Social Media Use

Patagonia uses social media to advocate for causes, prioritizing meaningful engagement over relentless promotion.

Pro Tip: Before opening an app, ask yourself: "What's my goal here?"

Exercise: Reflect on your digital habits and write down one intentional way to use technology this week.

PROTECT YOUR PRIVACY: ANCHOR IN TRUST

"Why worry about privacy? Everyone shares everything anyway," Kolaru shrugged.

"That's what they want you to think," Vaathi warned. "Privacy is power. Don't give it away."

In the digital world, your privacy is your anchor. Safeguarding your data gives you control over your digital identity.

Real Story: The Rise of Data Consciousness

Edward Snowden's revelations emphasized the importance of protecting personal information in a hyperconnected era.

Pro Tip: Use strong passwords, enable two-factor authentication, and be mindful of what you share online.

Exercise: Review your digital privacy settings and make at least one improvement this week.

LEVERAGE TECH FOR COLLABORATION

"I hate working with people online. It feels so distant," Kolaru grumbled.

"That's because you're doing it wrong," Vaathi said. "Tech can bridge distances if you use it well."

Technology breaks geographical barriers, enabling collaboration and innovation across distances.

Real Story: GitLab's Remote Success

GitLab operates entirely remotely, using digital tools to create seamless teamwork and productivity.

Pro Tip: Explore tools like Slack, Miro, or Trello to streamline collaboration.

Exercise: Try a new collaboration tool with your team and note its impact on productivity.

DISCONNECT TO RECONNECT: EMBRACE SILENCE

"I can't remember the last time I had a quiet moment," Kolaru said, rubbing his temples.

"That's because you're always plugged in," Vaathi replied. "Silence is where creativity and clarity live. Embrace it."

The constant buzz of notifications can drown out creativity and inner clarity. Regularly disconnecting helps you stay grounded.

Real Story: Cal Newport's Digital Minimalism

Author Cal Newport advocates for "digital decluttering," encouraging people to disconnect and focus on meaningful relationships and work.

Pro Tip: Practice a "digital detox" for a day or a weekend. Use the time to reflect, create, or connect offline.

Exercise: Schedule a digital detox period this week—even if it's just for a few hours.

USE AI AS YOUR ASSISTANT, NOT YOUR REPLACEMENT

"What if AI takes over everything?" Kolaru asked, eyes wide.

"It won't," Vaathi assured. "Because it lacks what makes you human—creativity, empathy, and intuition."

Artificial intelligence is a game-changer, but creativity, empathy, and innovation remain inherently human traits.

Real Story: AI in Creative Industries

AI tools streamline processes in industries like filmmaking and design, but the emotional depth and narrative heart of creativity remain uniquely human.

Pro Tip: Use AI to automate repetitive tasks, allowing more time for strategic and creative work.

Exercise: Identify one task you can automate using AI tools to free up time for meaningful work.

PRIORITIZE EMPATHY IN DIGITAL COMMUNICATION

"Emails feel so cold," Kolaru said. "How do you show empathy through a screen?"

"By choosing your words carefully," Vaathi replied. "And when it matters, use your voice."

Technology simplifies communication but often lacks emotional nuance. A human touch can bridge the gap.

Real Story: Empathy in Leadership

Satya Nadella emphasizes the importance of empathy in emails and virtual meetings, making digital interactions more meaningful.

Pro Tip: For sensitive topics, opt for voice or video calls rather than text or email.

Exercise: Replace one text or email this week with a voice or video call to add a personal touch.

TEACH THE NEXT GENERATION TO NAVIGATE TECH WISELY

"How do we stop kids from becoming screen zombies?" Kolaru asked.

"By teaching balance and leading by example," Vaathi replied. "They'll follow what you do, not what you say."

Equip the next wave with skills to use technology responsibly while fostering offline exploration and creativity.

Real Story: Parenting in the Digital Age

Melinda Gates emphasizes balanced tech use for children, promoting digital literacy while encouraging unplugged time for growth and imagination.

Pro Tip: Lead by example—model the digital habits you want younger generations to adopt.

Exercise: Have a family discussion about healthy tech use and agree on one new habit to implement together.

CLOSING CHALLENGE: FIND BALANCE ON THE DIGITAL WAVE

Technology is here to stay—and that's a good thing. It offers infinite opportunities for connection, learning, and creativity. But balance is essential to ensure it serves you, not vice versa. Harness its power, build connections, and innovate, all while staying rooted in your humanity.

"Your essence isn't digital," Vaathi said. "It's found in your kindness, creativity, and authenticity—qualities no app can replicate."

SURFING THE DIGITAL AGE WITH HUMANITY

Technology shapes the waves of the future, but your humanity is the anchor that keeps you grounded. Approach the digital tide with intention and balance, blending innovation with authenticity. The waves are rising, the future is calling—ride them with heart.

Kolaru (Excuses): "Why even bother at this point? It feels too late."

Vaathi (Truth): "Because if you stop now, everything you've learned goes to waste. Keep moving."

Building a Sustainable Future – Protecting the Ocean of Life

45

Life isn't just about surviving the present—it's about shaping a world where tomorrow flourishes. Every decision we make sends ripples across the ocean of life, influencing ecosystems, economies, and future generations. Sustainability isn't optional; it's the foundation for a future worth living.

The good news? Creating change doesn't require dramatic gestures. Your greatest weapon isn't just your voice; it's your wallet.

PURPOSEFUL PURCHASING: VOTE WITH YOUR WALLET

"Protests are pointless. Nobody listens," Kolaru scoffed.

"That's because you're screaming in the wrong language," Vaathi replied. "Money talks—louder than slogans ever will."

Forget slogans or protests—real change happens when consumers demand better. Every rupee or dollar you spend is a vote for the kind of world you want to see.

Example: Eco-friendly brands, from biodegradable packaging to clean energy solutions, thrive because consumers choose them. Global corporations are racing to go green, not because they care, but because people stopped accepting less.

Pro Tip: Before buying, ask: "Does this company's values align with mine?" Support those who prioritize sustainability.

Exercise: Reflect on a recent purchase. Did it align with your values? If not, what alternative could you choose next time?

SMALL CHOICES, BIG RIPPLES

"What difference does one person make?" Kolaru asked, skepticism dripping from every word.

"It's not about one choice," Vaathi said. "It's about thousands of small choices—ripples that become waves."

Change doesn't always require revolutions. Start small—switch off unused lights, shorten your showers, or replace single-use plastics. These small acts compound into a significant impact.

Example: Rainwater harvesting transformed water-scarce Indian villages without massive investments. Collective small actions rewrote the narrative.

Pro Tip: Mindful consumption matters. Ask yourself, "Do I need this, or am I buying for comfort?"

Exercise: Identify one small change you can make this week to reduce waste or conserve resources.

INNOVATION: A SMARTER TOMORROW

"Isn't sustainability just about going backward?" Kolaru frowned.

"No," Vaathi said firmly. "It's about going forward—smarter and more responsibly."

Sustainability isn't about going backward; it's about intelligent progress. Innovations like solar power and electric vehicles don't just save the planet—they fuel economic growth and create jobs.

Example: Tesla didn't just sell electric cars; it inspired an entire industry to rethink the future of transportation.

Pro Tip: Support businesses championing sustainability. Money spent on eco-friendly products fuels greener innovation.

Exercise: Research one innovative, sustainable product or service and share it with someone this week.

AMPLIFY IMPACT: EDUCATE AND INSPIRE

"Why should I care what others do?" Kolaru shrugged.

"Because change spreads," Vaathi replied. "Your actions inspire others. That's how revolutions begin."

Your choices matter, but inspiring others magnifies the ripple effect. Use your platform, whether it's social media or family conversations, to spread awareness.

Example: Plastic bans in Indian states began as grassroots campaigns—small conversations snowballed into legislative changes.

Pro Tip: Teach children sustainable habits. They're the next generation of consumers, and their choices will shape the future.

Exercise: Share one sustainability tip with your family or friends and encourage them to adopt it.

BIODIVERSITY: PROTECTING NATURE'S BALANCE

"Why does it matter if a few species go extinct?" Kolaru asked.

"Because every species plays a role," Vaathi explained. "Nature's balance is delicate. Pull one thread, and the entire fabric unravels."

Nature isn't just beautiful; it's vital. Every species plays a role in sustaining life's delicate equilibrium. Safeguarding biodiversity means preserving the systems that keep us alive.

Example: Reintroducing wolves to Yellowstone National Park stabilized the ecosystem, proving that every creature has a purpose.

Pro Tip: Support products and organizations that protect biodiversity. Shade-grown coffee, sustainable farming, or wildlife conservation efforts make a difference.

Exercise: Research one endangered species and learn how you can support its conservation.

COLLABORATION: STRENGTH IN NUMBERS

"I can't do this alone," Kolaru sighed.

"You're not supposed to," Vaathi said with a smile. "Join forces with others. Together, we're unstoppable."

You're not alone in this mission. Partner with like-minded individuals, organizations, or brands to amplify your efforts.

Example: Mumbai's Versova Beach cleanup wasn't the work of one hero—it was the collective effort of hundreds, transforming a garbage-strewn coast into a thriving shoreline.

Pro Tip: Progress isn't about perfection; it's about momentum. Every small action contributes to a larger impact.

Exercise: Identify an organization or group focused on sustainability and explore how you can collaborate or contribute.

SYSTEMS, NOT SHORT-TERM FIXES

"Quick fixes are easier," Kolaru said.

"And they don't last," Vaathi countered. "Build systems for lasting change."

Band-Aids solve immediate problems, but sustainable systems create lasting change. Circular economies, where waste becomes a resource, represent the future.

Example: Kerala's waste segregation program didn't just clean up streets—it became a blueprint for sustainable living across India.

Pro Tip: Think long-term. A single reusable bottle saves hundreds of plastic ones from landfills.

Exercise: Implement one system in your daily life to reduce waste or conserve resources.

LEGACY: A WORLD WORTH INHERITING

"What's the point of all this?" Kolaru asked, frustration evident.

"Legacy," Vaathi said softly. "Imagine a future where clean air and thriving forests are the norm. That's the world you can help create."

Imagine a future where clean air and thriving forests are the norm. That's the legacy you have the power to leave—not through grand gestures but consistent, meaningful actions.

Witty **Insight:** Legacy isn't a statue with your name; it's a better world your children don't have to rebuild.

Pro Tip: Don't aim for perfection. Aim for progress and inspire others to continue the journey.

Exercise: Write down one action you'll take this month to contribute to a sustainable future.

SUSTAINABILITY AS A PRIVILEGE

Sustainability isn't a burden; it's an opportunity to protect the ocean of life. Every decision you make shapes the future, and small, intentional acts can create ripples of meaningful change.

Pro Tip: Money speaks louder than protests. Spend wisely, live purposefully, and watch your choices transform the world.

RIDING THE WAVES OF SUSTAINABILITY

The ocean of life is ours to protect—not deplete. Together, we can build a future where humanity and nature thrive in harmony. The waves of tomorrow call for action today. Will you answer?

46

FACING NEW FRONTIERS – EMBRACING UNCERTAINTY WITH CURIOSITY

Life is an endless ocean, brimming with opportunities and mysteries. Every new frontier is an invitation to explore, to ride waves that challenge your skills and expand your perspective. The currents may be unfamiliar, the waters unpredictable, but isn't that what makes the journey exhilarating?

Facing the future with curiosity instead of fear is the ultimate act of bravery. It's not about knowing every answer; it's about asking the right questions and daring to discover. Frontiers are more than physical; they stretch across emotions, intellect, and spirit, inviting you to evolve.

This chapter delves into the art of embracing uncertainty, turning hesitation into wonder, and charting paths that inspire others to follow.

EVERY FRONTIER STARTS AS UNKNOWN WATERS

"Why should I dive into the unknown? What if I drown?" Kolaru asked, nervously tapping his fingers.

Vaathi gave a calm, knowing smile. "The unknown is where everything new begins. Staying on the shore guarantees nothing but stagnation. The ocean might surprise you."

Uncertainty isn't a barrier but a gateway to possibility. Every breakthrough begins with a question: "What lies beyond?"

Real Story: Christopher Columbus didn't have a map of the Atlantic. What he had was curiosity, which fueled an exploration that reshaped history.

Pro Tip: Replace fear of the unknown with excitement for discovery. Ask, "What can I learn?" or "What might surprise me?"

Exercise: Reflect on a time you avoided something because it felt unfamiliar. What would have changed if you had approached it with curiosity?

PREPARE, BUT DON'T OVERPREPARE

"I'll go once I have every detail planned," Kolaru insisted.

Vaathi shook his head. "Waves don't wait for your perfect plan. If you hesitate too long, you'll miss the ride."

Preparation is vital, but overplanning can stall your momentum. Waves reward adaptability and courage, not rigidity.

Real Story: Apollo 11. The Apollo 11 astronauts prepared rigorously, yet their success depended as much on their adaptability during unplanned moments as on their training.

Pro Tip: Plan what you can, but leave room for improvisation. Trust your instincts when the unexpected arises.

Exercise: Write down one area where you've overprepared in the past. How can you embrace flexibility in future plans?

CURIOSITY: YOUR COMPASS IN THE UNKNOWN

"What if I fail?" Kolaru asked.

"What if you succeed?" Vaathi countered. "Curiosity flips the question. It turns fear into wonder."

Curiosity transforms uncertainty into opportunity. It shifts the narrative from "What if I fail?" to "What can I learn?"

Real Story: Jane Goodall's groundbreaking work with chimpanzees began with her insatiable curiosity. It led to discoveries that changed how humanity sees itself.

Pro Tip: Adopt a beginner's mindset. Ask questions without fear of appearing uninformed. Curiosity opens doors.

Exercise: Think of a question you've been afraid to ask. Write it down and commit to finding the answer.

COLLABORATE: SHARED FRONTIERS ARE LESS DAUNTING

"Why face the unknown alone?" Kolaru questioned.

Vaathi nodded. "Exactly. Find allies. Shared journeys are lighter and richer."

Exploration is easier—and more rewarding with allies. Collaboration fosters courage, innovation, and shared success.

Real Story: The Human Genome Project. Scientists worldwide united to decode life's blueprint, proving that shared efforts conquer even the most daunting challenges.

Pro Tip: Surround yourself with diverse perspectives. Seek mentors, teammates, or communities that challenge and inspire you.

Exercise: Identify one person who could help you navigate an unknown area. Reach out to them this week.

EXPERIMENT FEARLESSLY

"I hate failing," Kolaru admitted.

"Then you hate learning," Vaathi replied bluntly. "Progress is built on trial and error. Each experiment is a step forward."

Progress is rarely linear. It's built through trial, error, and resilience. Each experiment teaches you what works and what doesn't.

Real Story: Thomas Edison's journey to invent the lightbulb included thousands of failed attempts, each one a step closer to success.

Pro Tip: Redefine failure as feedback. Each setback is a lesson in disguise.

Exercise: List one area where you've avoided taking risks. Commit to one small experiment this week.

LEAVE A TRAIL FOR OTHERS TO FOLLOW

"Why share my struggles?" Kolaru asked. "No one cares."

"You'd be surprised," Vaathi said gently. "Your journey could light the way for someone else."

Your journey into the unknown doesn't end with you. Sharing your experiences creates a path for others, inspiring them to explore their own frontiers.

Real Story: Maya Angelou's autobiographies didn't just recount her life—they became maps of resilience, courage, and authenticity for millions.

Pro Tip: Document and share your insights openly. Your story could be the spark someone else needs.

Exercise: Write down one lesson you've learned from facing the unknown. Share it with someone this week.

CLOSING CHALLENGE: EMBRACE THE FRONTIER

The unknown isn't a threat—it's an invitation. Every new frontier, whether in your career, relationships, or personal growth, holds the promise of discovery. Step boldly into it with curiosity as your compass and resilience as your anchor.

"Your future self is waiting," Vaathi said. "Don't keep them waiting."

Pro Tip: The future belongs to the explorers—those who dare to paddle out into uncharted waters.

Exercise: Reflect on a decision you've been avoiding. What's one small step you can take today to face it head-on?

THE FRONTIER OF POSSIBILITY

The horizon is infinite, and the waves of opportunity are endless. To ride them, you need curiosity to paddle out, courage to catch them, and resilience to stay balanced.

The next frontier is waiting—not to be conquered but to be experienced, shared, and celebrated. So, what's your next wave? Paddle out, explore, and leave a legacy that inspires others to follow.

47

ENDLESS SURF – EMBRACING LIFELONG LEARNING

Learning isn't a destination—it's a continuous journey across an infinite ocean. Each wave brings lessons, and just as you master one, another appears on the horizon. To live fully is to embrace this endless surf, nurturing curiosity, resilience, and humility.

The most impactful individuals—whether artists, scientists, or leaders—never stop learning. They understand that knowledge is vast, and every experience, no matter how small, holds the potential to teach. This chapter explores how to ride the waves of lifelong learning with grace and joy.

LEARNING NEVER ENDS: IT'S AN INFINITE OCEAN

"The ocean doesn't run out of waves, and life doesn't run out of lessons," Vaathi said, his gaze steady. "But some people prefer to sit on the shore, complaining about the tide."

Kolaru smirked. "Well, sitting is easier."

"And you learn nothing," Vaathi retorted. "The choice is yours—ride the waves or let them drown you."

The ocean doesn't run out of waves, and life doesn't run out of lessons. Learning is the essence of growth, not just a phase.

Real Story: Leonardo da Vinci spent his life exploring art, anatomy, engineering, and botany. His insatiable curiosity fueled innovations that shaped history.

Pro Tip: Treat each day as an opportunity to learn. Every experience, conversation, or challenge contains valuable lessons.

Exercise: Reflect on a decision where the timing was off and strategize a better timing for future decisions.

ADOPT A BEGINNER'S MINDSET

"So, you're saying I should pretend I know nothing?" Kolaru asked.

Vaathi shook his head. "Not pretend. Accept it. There's power in admitting you don't know—it opens the door to learning."

A beginner's mindset means releasing assumptions and remaining open to new possibilities. It's the humility to say, "I don't know—yet."

Real Story: Socrates' declaration, "I know that I know nothing," became the foundation of his lifelong quest for wisdom.

Pro Tip: Approach familiar situations as if you're encountering them for the first time. Ask "Why?" even when you think you know the answer.

Exercise: Reflect on a decision where the timing was off and strategize a better timing for future decisions.

REFLECT TO CONNECT THE DOTS

"I don't have time to reflect," Kolaru grumbled.

"You don't have time not to," Vaathi countered. "Without reflection, you're just repeating mistakes and calling it progress."

Reflection transforms learning into wisdom. It helps you connect experiences, recognize patterns, and extract deeper insights.

Real Story: Albert Einstein attributed much of his genius to quiet reflection, stating, "I think 99 times and find nothing. I stop thinking, swim in silence, and the truth comes to me."

Pro Tip: Make journaling a habit. Writing down your thoughts helps you process and internalize your lessons.

Exercise: Reflect on a decision where the timing was off and strategize a better timing for future decisions.

EXPERIMENT FEARLESSLY—MISTAKES ARE LESSONS

"I hate making mistakes," Kolaru admitted.

"Then you hate learning," Vaathi replied. "Mistakes are the universe's way of teaching you."

Mistakes aren't failures; they're stepping stones. Lifelong learners embrace experimentation, knowing that every misstep reveals new insights.

Real Story: James Dyson built 5,127 prototypes before perfecting his vacuum cleaner, learning from each iteration.

Pro Tip: Replace the fear of failure with excitement for discovery. Celebrate what mistakes teach you.

Exercise: Reflect on a decision where the timing was off and strategize a better timing for future decisions.

SEEK DIVERSE SOURCES—EVERYTHING AND EVERYONE IS A TEACHER

"I've already read enough," Kolaru said. "What more is there to learn?"

Vaathi chuckled. "Books are great. But life is the ultimate teacher. People, nature, even failures—they all have lessons if you're willing to listen."

The best learners draw from diverse sources: books, people, nature, and personal experiences. Cross-disciplinary learning sparks creativity and innovation.

Real Story: Steve Jobs credited a calligraphy class with inspiring Apple's focus on elegant typography, which became a hallmark of its brand.

Pro Tip: Step outside your comfort zone. Explore fields and perspectives that differ from your own.

Exercise: Reflect on a decision where the timing was off and strategize a better timing for future decisions.

TEACHING DEEPENS LEARNING

"Why should I teach someone else? I'm still figuring things out myself," Kolaru protested.

"Teaching is how you figure things out," Vaathi explained. "It forces you to clarify your thoughts."

Teaching what you've learned clarifies your understanding and amplifies your impact. Sharing knowledge creates ripples of growth.

Real Story: Richard Feynman believed in simplifying complex ideas, saying, "If you can't explain it simply, you don't understand it well enough."

Pro Tip: Teach someone what you've recently learned. The process will reveal gaps and deepen your comprehension.

Exercise: Reflect on a decision where the timing was off and strategize a better timing for future decisions.

STAY HUMBLE—THE MORE YOU LEARN, THE MORE YOU REALIZE YOU DON'T KNOW

"I hate not knowing things," Kolaru said.

"Good," Vaathi replied. "That's the first step to wisdom. The moment you think you know everything, you've stopped learning."

Lifelong learners embrace humility, knowing that every wave reveals deeper unknowns.

Real Story: Marie Curie, despite her groundbreaking discoveries, remained humble, acknowledging the vast mysteries still to be unraveled.

Pro Tip: Celebrate what you don't know—it's fuel for future growth.

Exercise: Reflect on a decision where the timing was off and strategize a better timing for future decisions.

CELEBRATE PROGRESS—EVERY WAVE COUNTS

"But I haven't mastered anything," Kolaru sighed.

"Mastery isn't the goal," Vaathi said. "Progress is. Celebrate each wave you ride—big or small."

Lifelong learning isn't about mastering everything; it's about progress. Celebrate even the smallest milestones—they build momentum for the journey ahead.

Real Story: Nelson Mandela, who learned to read and write during imprisonment, viewed small victories as stepping stones toward freedom.

Pro Tip: Track your growth. Acknowledge and reward yourself for each step forward.

Exercise: Reflect on a decision where the timing was off and strategize a better timing for future decisions.

CLOSING CHALLENGE: RIDE THE ENDLESS WAVE

Learning has no finish line. It's a perpetual ride across an infinite ocean, with each wave offering new perspectives and skills. Embrace curiosity, practice humility, and approach each day as a student of life.

Pro Tip: Lifelong learning isn't about achieving mastery—it's about enjoying the process.

Exercise: Reflect on a decision where the timing was off and strategize a better timing for future decisions.

THE JOY OF LIFELONG LEARNING

The greatest gift you can give yourself is the freedom to keep learning. To paddle out into the ocean of knowledge, ride waves of curiosity, and embrace the beauty of not knowing—that's what makes life endlessly rich and rewarding.

So, what's your next wave of learning? The ocean is vast, the waves are infinite, and the possibilities are boundless. Paddle out, dive in, and let curiosity guide you to new horizons.

STYLE IN CHAOS – RIDING LIFE'S FINAL WAVE WITH PANACHE

48

THE FINAL WAVE: A SIGNATURE RIDE

Life is an ocean—boundless, unpredictable, and full of wonder. Each of us is a surfer, navigating its tides and currents with courage and creativity. The final wave isn't about endings—it's the culmination of all the waves you've ridden, the lessons you've learned, and the mark you leave behind.

This chapter celebrates style in chaos—the art of embracing life's last moments with dignity, humor, and authenticity. As with every wave you've faced, it's not the size of the wave that matters but how you choose to ride it.

LIFE'S FINAL WAVE IS A RIPPLE, NOT A STOP

Kolaru leaned back, arms crossed. "So, what's the point? It all ends anyway."

Vaathi's gaze didn't waver. "It's not about endings. It's about the ripples you leave behind."

The journey doesn't end when the wave reaches the shore. Your actions, values, and lessons ripple outward, influencing others long after you've moved on.

Real Story: Think of Mahatma Gandhi's enduring legacy. His life wasn't about grand finales but about ripples of peace and justice that continue to inspire movements around the world.

Pro Tip: Focus on the impact you've made, not the waves you've missed. Your influence lives on through the people and values you've touched.

Exercise: Reflect on one action that created a positive ripple in someone else's life. How can you continue to spread those ripples?

LEAVE WITH STYLE: YOUR JOURNEY IS YOUR SIGNATURE

"So, I need a grand farewell?" Kolaru smirked.

"Not at all," Vaathi replied. "It's the everyday moments that define your legacy, not the dramatic exits."

The way you ride your final wave defines your legacy. Choose to end with authenticity, dignity, and flair.

Real Story: J.R.D. Tata retired from the Tata Group with quiet grace and continued mentorship, ensuring that his vision thrived through those he inspired.

Pro Tip: Don't chase a grand finale. Live with intention every day so your legacy becomes a collection of meaningful moments.

Exercise: Write down three values you want to be remembered for. How can you embody them daily?

REFLECT, CELEBRATE, AND SHARE YOUR STORY

Kolaru scratched his head. "Why bother sharing? Nobody cares."

Vaathi raised an eyebrow. "Your story isn't just for you. It's a map for others finding their way."

Your life is a unique narrative. Reflect on its highs and lows, celebrate its lessons, and share your story to inspire others.

Real Story: Maya Angelou's memoirs didn't just recount her life; they taught resilience, courage, and the transformative power of storytelling.

Pro Tip: Reflect without judgment. The lows have shaped you as much as the highs.

Exercise: Write down one lesson from a challenging experience. Share it with someone who might benefit from your insight.

EMBRACE GRATITUDE: YOUR FINAL LEGACY

"Gratitude? Sounds cheesy," Kolaru muttered.

Vaathi smiled. "Cheesy? Maybe. Powerful? Absolutely. Gratitude turns endings into celebrations."

Gratitude transforms endings into celebrations. It honors the people, experiences, and waves that have shaped your life.

Real Story: The Dalai Lama's enduring message of gratitude and compassion has inspired countless movements for peace.

Pro Tip: Gratitude isn't just about the past—it's about recognizing the beauty of the present moment.

Exercise: List five people or experiences you're grateful for. Reach out to at least one and express your gratitude.

STAY HUMOROUS: LIGHTNESS IN THE WAVES

"Life's too serious to joke around," Kolaru said.

Vaathi laughed. "No. Life's too unpredictable to take it seriously all the time."

A sense of humor is a surfer's secret weapon, helping you ride even the toughest waves with resilience and perspective.

Real Story: Comedian Robin Williams, despite his personal struggles, used humor to uplift millions. His legacy reminds us that laughter can leave lasting ripples.

Pro Tip: Don't take life—or yourself—too seriously. The best waves are the ones you enjoy.

Exercise: Recall a moment when humor helped you navigate a tough situation. How can you bring more lightness into your daily life?

TRUST THE RIPPLE EFFECT

"How do I know my efforts matter?" Kolaru asked.

"You don't," Vaathi said simply. "You trust that they do."

As you ride life's final wave, trust that the ripples you've created will inspire, uplift, and guide others.

Real Story: Dr. Abdul Kalam's life of simplicity and service inspired countless students to dream big, proving that quiet ripples often create the loudest impact.

Pro Tip: Let go of control. Trust that the waves you've created will reach distant shores.

Exercise: Write down one value or lesson you've shared with someone. Reflect on how it might influence their future.

APPRECIATE THE INFINITE HORIZON

"What if this is the end?" Kolaru asked softly.

"The end of one wave is the beginning of another," Vaathi replied. "The horizon is infinite."

The end of one wave is the beginning of another. Life's mystery lies in its infinite possibilities, even as one chapter closes.

Real Story: Carl Sagan's Pale Blue Dot reminds us of the vastness of existence, inspiring curiosity and humility about our place in the universe.

Pro Tip: The horizon isn't fixed. Every ending opens new possibilities, even if they're not yet visible.

Exercise: Imagine your next chapter. What new wave are you excited to ride?

CLOSING CHALLENGE: RIDE WITH STYLE AND GRACE

Life's final wave isn't about avoiding wipeouts but about riding with courage, wisdom, and flair. Your legacy isn't built on grand gestures but on the authenticity and impact of your everyday moments.

Pro Tip: Style isn't about perfection; it's about riding the wave your way.

Exercise: Reflect on a moment when you handled chaos with grace. How can you bring that same style to future challenges?

WRAP-UP: THE ENDLESS HORIZON

As this book closes, remember that life's lessons are infinite, just like the ocean. Adaptability, learning, and style are your tools to navigate each wave, whether calm or chaotic.

The horizon isn't an end—it's a reminder of new beginnings, fresh opportunities, and infinite possibilities. Paddle out, ride boldly, and leave your mark with purpose, courage, and flair. The ocean is vast, but your waves—no matter their size—will always be felt.

FINAL REFLECTION: THE ENDLESS HORIZON AWAITS

Kolaru stood at the **water's edge**, the cool sand shifting under his feet as he stared at the **horizon**. The waves rolled in, steady and endless.

Vaathi approached, standing beside him. **"Lost in thought again?"**

Kolaru nodded, his voice quieter than usual. **"Just wondering if I've missed too many waves in my life."**

Vaathi smirked, eyes on the ocean. **"Missed waves don't matter, Kolaru. It's the ones you choose to ride that define you."**

Kolaru let out a half-laugh, half-sigh. **"But what if I wiped out all the important ones?"** He kicked a pebble into the surf, watching the ripples spread.

"Then you've learned more than most people ever will," Vaathi said. **"Wipeouts aren't failures—they're lessons. The real failure is standing on the shore, blaming the ocean for being unpredictable."**

Kolaru raised an eyebrow. **"Easy for you to say. But how do you even know which wave is worth the risk?"**

Vaathi shrugged. "You don't. And that's the point. Life isn't about certainty—it's about curiosity. Paddle into the unknown, fall, rise again, adapt. That's where the growth is."

Kolaru sighed. **"What if the next wave is my last?"**

Vaathi chuckled. **"Then ride it with style. Leave a ripple that reaches shores far beyond your sight. Legacy isn't about how long you ride—it's about how deeply you touch others."**

For a moment, they stood in **silence**, the crashing waves filling the space.

FEARING THE HORIZON

"Why do you think people fear the horizon?" Kolaru asked.

Vaathi's gaze remained steady. **"Because it's endless. It reflects what they fear most—uncertainty. But that same endlessness is what makes it beautiful. Every wave brings a new possibility."**

Kolaru smirked. **"And here I thought you'd talk about fate or destiny."**

Vaathi laughed. **"Destiny is just a fancy word for the choices we justify in hindsight. What matters is the decision you make right now. The horizon will always be there, waiting."**

Kolaru tilted his head. **"So, what's the lesson in all this?"**

Vaathi stepped into the surf, letting the water lap at his feet. **"The lesson is simple: stop waiting. Stop fearing. Stop doubting. Paddle out, ride the wave, and make your mark."**

Kolaru hesitated for a second, then followed him into the water. **"And if I wipe out again?"**

"Then get back on the board." Vaathi's voice was firm. **"The ocean doesn't care how many times you fall. It only cares that you show up."**

WHAT COMES NEXT?

Later, as the sun dipped low, painting the sky **gold and crimson**, Kolaru leaned back in his chair thoughtfully.

"Vaathi, we've covered everything—from self-mastery to leadership, riding chaos, and even legacy. So… what's next?"

Vaathi smiled, eyes on the **horizon. "Now you surf."**

Kolaru frowned. **"That's it? You're saying the whole point is to just keep going?"**

"Not just going, Kolaru. Going with style." Vaathi turned to face him. **"Riding life's waves isn't enough. Do it with clarity, grace, and purpose— that's style."**

Kolaru grinned. **"Style, huh? Is that why you dragged me through all those chapters on mindfulness, influence, and building a compass?"**

Vaathi nodded. **"Exactly. Style isn't about being flawless. It's about showing up as yourself, every single time—whether the waters are calm or chaotic."**

Kolaru's grin faded slightly. **"But what if I fail again?"**

Vaathi met his gaze. **"Then you get back on the board. Every fall shapes you, Kolaru. Every wave teaches you."**

Kolaru exhaled slowly. **"And the unknown? It still scares me."**

Vaathi leaned forward. **"Good. Fear means you're alive. But don't let it stop you. Courage isn't about being fearless—it's about acting despite the fear. The unknown isn't your enemy—it's where growth happens."**

THE POINT OF IT ALL

Kolaru chuckled. **"Alright, we've talked about surfing, legacy, leadership… even memes. But you never really answered the big question."**

"Which is?" Vaathi asked.

Kolaru leaned forward. **"What's the point of all this? Why bother learning all these lessons if life's just going to throw more waves?"**

Vaathi's eyes twinkled. **"Because knowledge isn't enough. Wisdom is motion. It's not about what you know—it's about what you do with it. The point is to live it."**

Kolaru nodded slowly. **"So… I'm free to go?"**

Vaathi smiled. **"Yes. You're free to go."**

But Kolaru didn't move. He sat quietly, then shook his head. **"I'm not ready yet. Not until I've ridden a few more waves."**

Vaathi's grin widened. **"Good. Because the ocean is waiting. And the waves are rising."**

As Kolaru stood, the **horizon** stretched endlessly before him—a canvas of **infinite possibility**. He turned back one last time. **"What if I forget all this?"**

Vaathi laughed. **"You won't. Because wisdom isn't in what you read—it's in what you live. Every wave you ride will remind you."**

Kolaru saluted, his grin infectious. **"See you out there, Vaathi."**

Vaathi watched him walk toward the **horizon,** a smile lingering. **"See you out there, Kolaru. And remember—surf with style."**

Wisdom is Endless

This book is a mosaic of ideas, insights, and reflections shaped by the brilliance of those who came before me. These authors and their works have been like torchlights, illuminating paths I needed to walk. They didn't just inspire me—they equipped me with tools, perspectives, and questions that shaped my thinking and writing.

Here are the works that have resonated deeply with the themes of this book. If any of the ideas in these chapters have sparked something within you, I encourage you to explore these works directly. The wisdom they carry is boundless, and this book is but one stop along the endless river of knowledge.

PERSONAL DEVELOPMENT & SELF-DISCOVERY

- The 5 Second Rule by Mel Robbins – For breaking free from procrastination and turning hesitation into action.

- Inner Engineering by Sadhguru – For balancing the inner and outer world with practical insights.

- The Compound Effect by Darren Hardy – For showing the power of small, consistent actions over time.

- 12 Rules for Life by Jordan B. Peterson – For blending timeless wisdom with practical living.

- Models by Mark Manson – For redefining self-improvement with honesty and clarity.

LEADERSHIP, INFLUENCE & CONNECTION

- Flawless Consulting by Peter Block – For redefining trust and professionalism in leadership.

- Start with Why by Simon Sinek – For understanding the power of purpose and inspiration.

- Never Split the Difference by Chris Voss – For mastering negotiation through empathy and connection.
- The Trusted Advisor by David H. Maister – For building trust and credibility in every interaction.

MINDSET, CREATIVITY & RESILIENCE

- Think Again by Adam Grant – For teaching the art of rethinking and adaptability.
- Never Finished by David Goggins – For showing that limits are an illusion and resilience is a choice.
- The Subtle Art of Not Giving a F*ck by Mark Manson – For focusing on what truly matters in life.

STORYTELLING & COMMUNICATION

- Storytelling with Data by Cole Nussbaumer Knaflic – For turning complex ideas into powerful stories.
- Steal Like an Artist by Austin Kleon – For unlocking creativity by embracing influence and curiosity.

CRITICAL THINKING & ADAPTABILITY

- Your Deceptive Mind by Steven Novella – For fostering critical thinking and skepticism.
- The Digital Transformation Playbook by David L. Rogers – For navigating change in a fast-evolving world.

This book is my offering to the river of wisdom that has flowed through centuries, carrying the thoughts of those who dared to think, question, and create. To the authors and their works, my deepest gratitude. To you, my readers, this is your invitation to join the journey—seek, learn, and share.

Wisdom is endless, and so is the journey.

About the Author

Kottai Chezhiyan—known to his close circle as **Chezy**—isn't your everyday storyteller. He's the kind of guy who skips the small talk and dives straight into the questions that stick with you long after the conversation ends. He doesn't settle for surface-level answers or cookie-cutter solutions; instead, he's all about unraveling the patterns of chaos to uncover life's hidden truths.

Professionally, Chezy has spent years as a finance leader, not just crunching numbers but reading between the lines to find the stories buried in data. But the real magic happens outside the spreadsheets, where his fascination with life, behavior, and human nature takes center stage. For Chezy, the chaos of life isn't a problem to solve—it's a dance to master.

His philosophy? Life's challenges aren't solo battles; they're collective symphonies. Growing up, when his family faced unexpected storms, Chezy learned that resilience is rooted in togetherness, in the grit to move forward, and the wisdom to let go. That belief became his compass, guiding him to embrace life's unpredictable waves with both clarity and style.

Influenced by everyone, from scientists and entrepreneurs to monks and filmmakers, Chezy has crafted a philosophy that's uniquely his own. It's simple: cut the fluff, focus on what matters, and apply the damn lesson. He draws inspiration from books, movies, and personal experiences to share insights that are practical, timeless, and brutally honest.

When he's not coaching teams or unraveling life's puzzles, you'll find Chezy sipping chai, playing anonymous chess matches online, or hitting the road on a long drive—always curious, always seeking new patterns in the chaos.

This book isn't just a collection of ideas; it's a call to action. Crafted with the hope of making the world at least 0.1% better, it's an invitation to embrace the unknown, confront reality, and find your own rhythm in the chaos.

Because, as Chezy would say, "If you're going to surf the waves, do it with style—or don't bother at all." An praveres nonvenistrae et res aut verunum coentid eorat. morum egili, utus, sit C. Imulvir liure hae it.